EASY PIANO | 2ND EDITION

Easy Broadway

ISBN 978-0-7935-3829-4

HAL•LEONARD®
CORPORATION
7777 W. BLUEMOUND RD. P.O. BOX 13819 MILWAUKEE, WI 53213

Visit Hal Leonard Online at
www.halleonard.com

ALL I ASK OF YOU

from THE PHANTOM OF THE OPERA

Music by ANDREW LLOYD WEBBER
Lyrics by CHARLES HART
Additional Lyrics by RICHARD STILGOE

Slowly, in 2
RAOUL:

With pedal

No more talk of dark-ness, for-get these wide-eyed

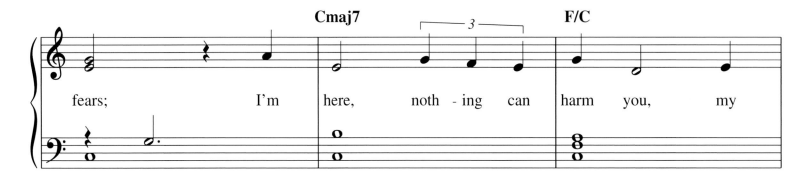

fears; I'm here, noth-ing can harm you, my

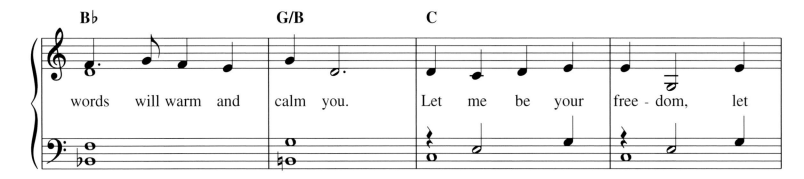

words will warm and calm you. Let me be your free-dom, let

day-light dry your tears; I'm here, with you, be-

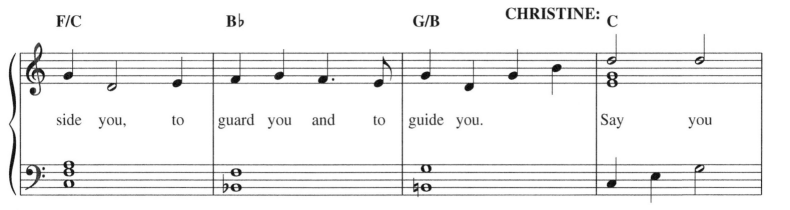

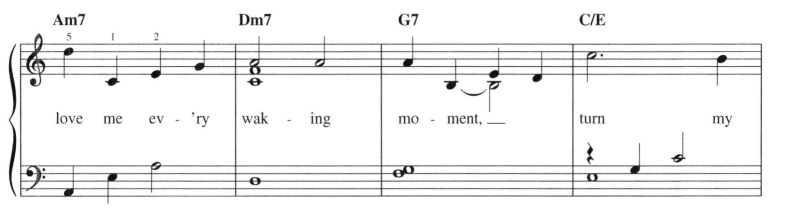

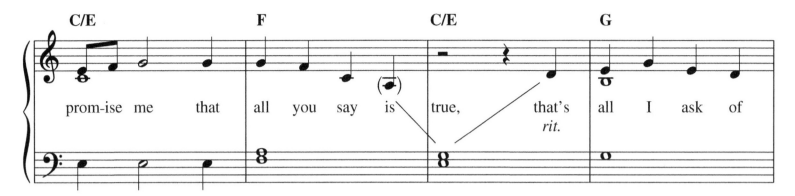

C/E   **F**   **C/E**   **G**

prom-ise me that all you say is true, that's all I ask of

rit.

RAOUL:

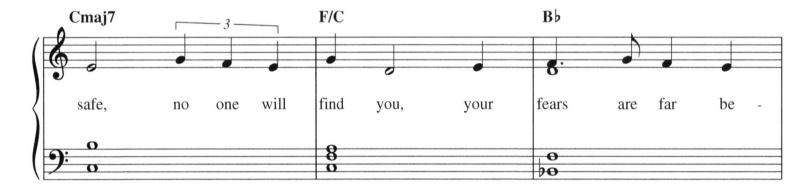

C

mf

Let me be your shel - ter, let me be your light; you're

you.

a tempo

Cmaj7   **F/C**   **B♭**

safe, no one will find you, your fears are far be -

CHRISTINE:

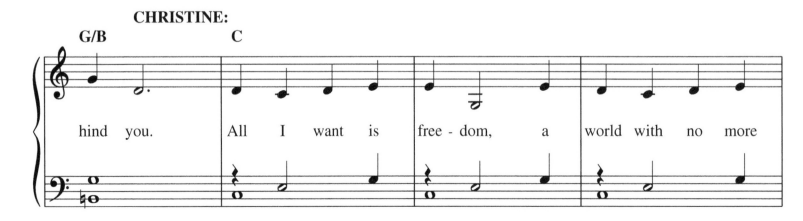

G/B   **C**

hind you. All I want is free - dom, a world with no more

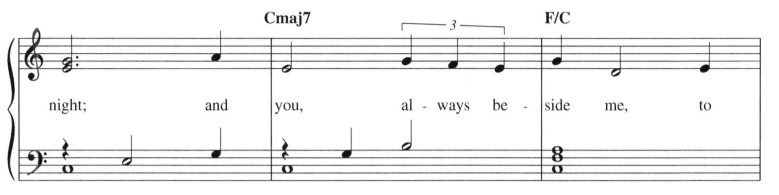

night; and you, al - ways be - side me, to

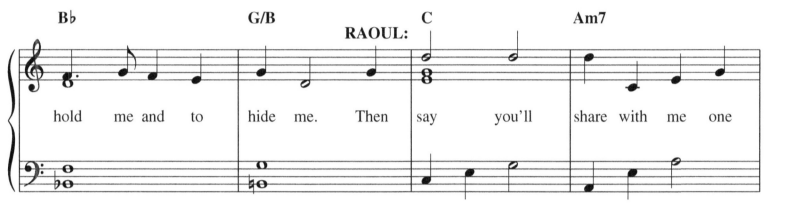

hold me and to hide me. **RAOUL:** Then say you'll share with me one

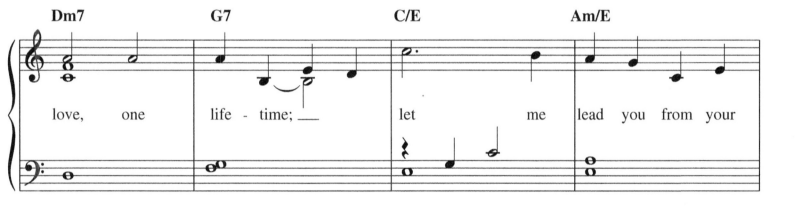

love, one life - time; ___ let me lead you from your

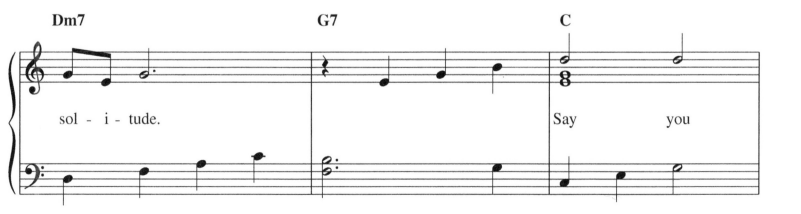

sol - i - tude. Say you

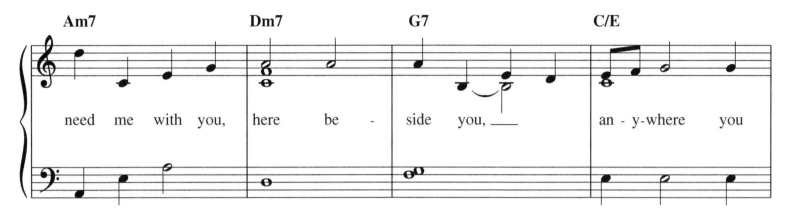

need me with you, here be - side you, ___ an - y-where you

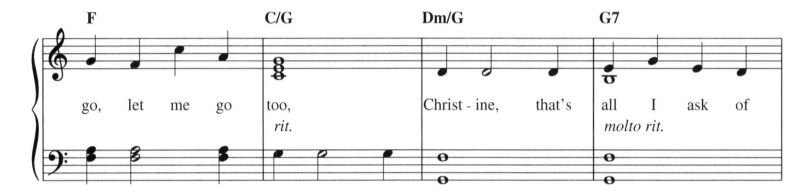

go, let me go too, Christ - ine, that's all I ask of
rit. *molto rit.*

CHRISTINE:

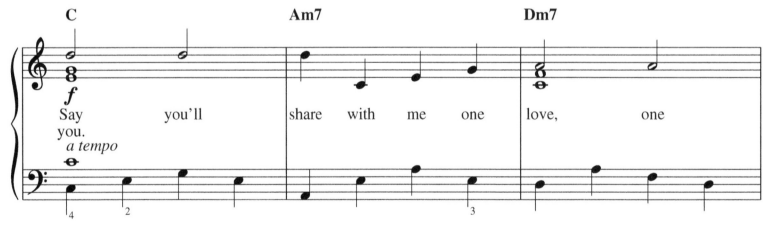

Say you'll share with me one love, one
you.
a tempo

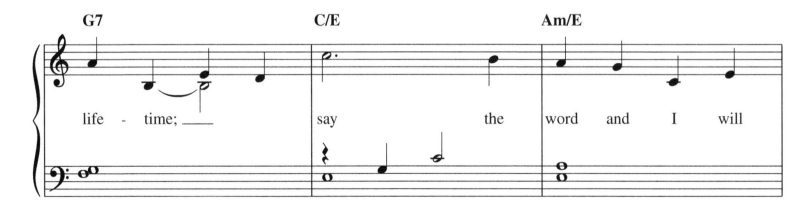

life - time; ___ say the word and I will

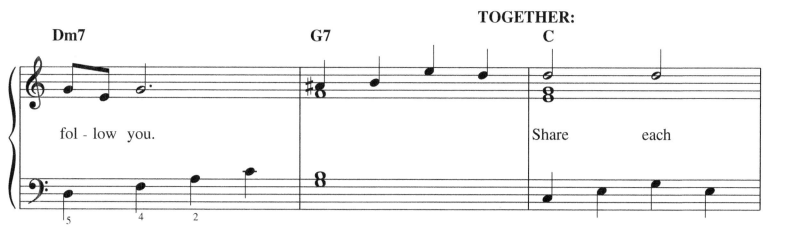

TOGETHER:

fol - low you. Share each

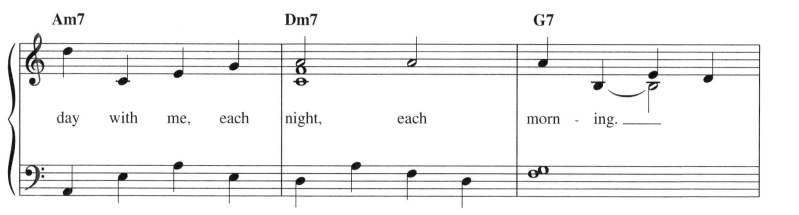

day with me, each night, each morn - ing. ____

Slower

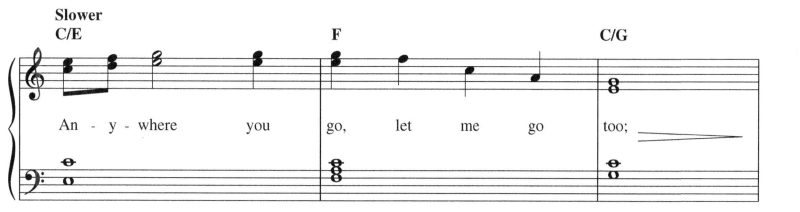

An - y - where you go, let me go too;

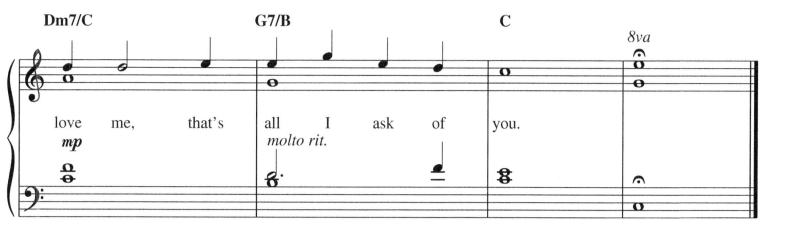

love me, that's all I ask of you.

mp   *molto rit.*

BRING HIM HOME

from LES MISÉRABLES

Music by CLAUDE-MICHEL SCHÖNBERG
Lyrics by ALAIN BOUBLIL and HERBERT KRETZMER

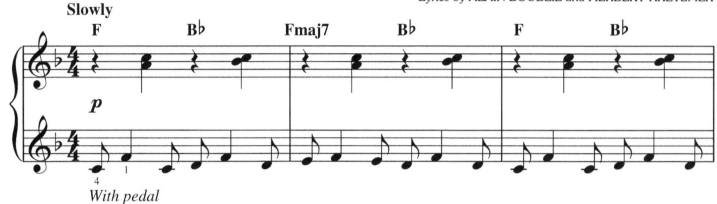

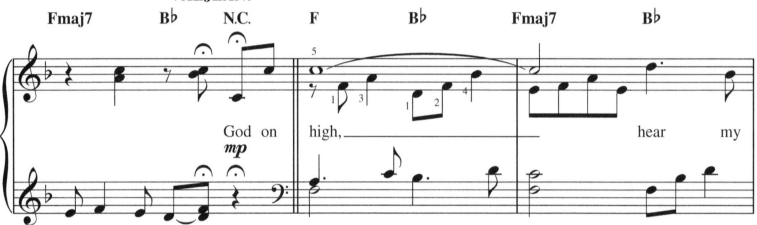

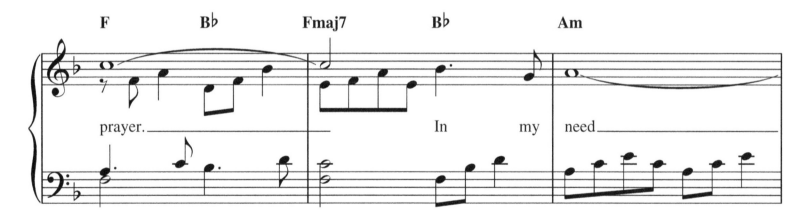

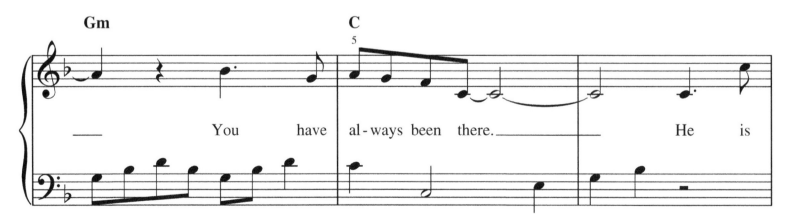

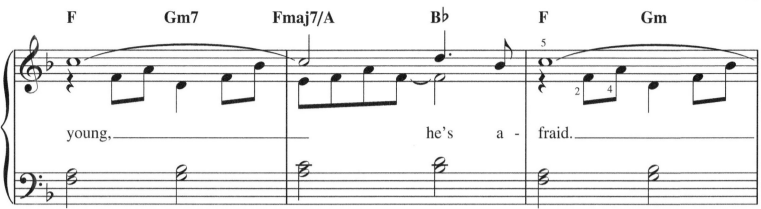

young, _____ he's a - fraid. _____

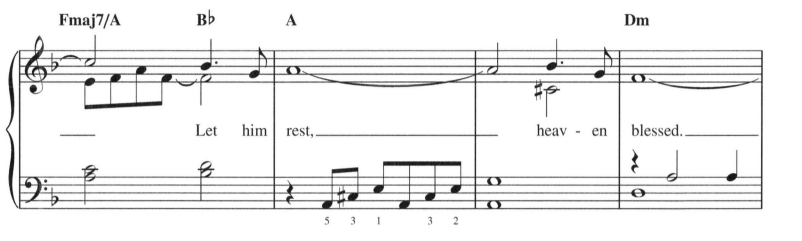

_____ Let him rest, _____ heav - en blessed. _____

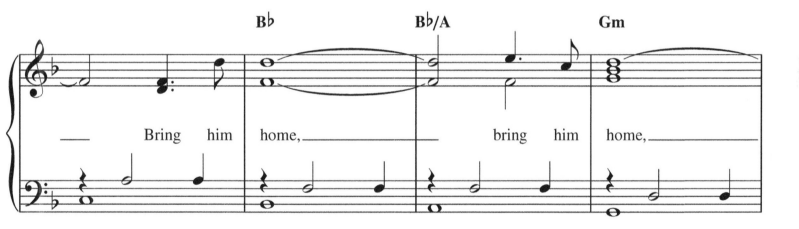

_____ Bring him home, _____ bring him home, _____

A bit faster

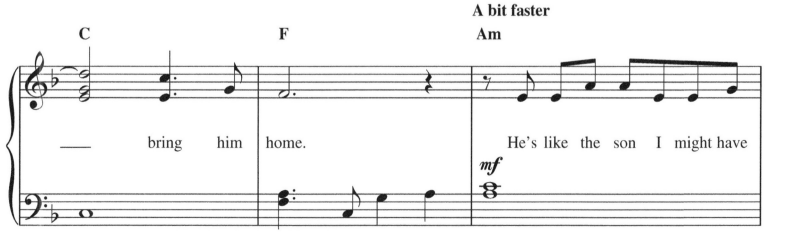

_____ bring him home. He's like the son I might have

known ___ if God had grant-ed me a son. The sum-mers

die ___ one by one. How soon they fly ___ on and on. And I am

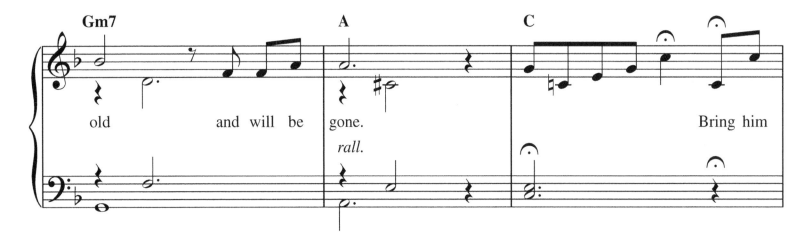

old ___ and will be gone. *rall.* Bring him

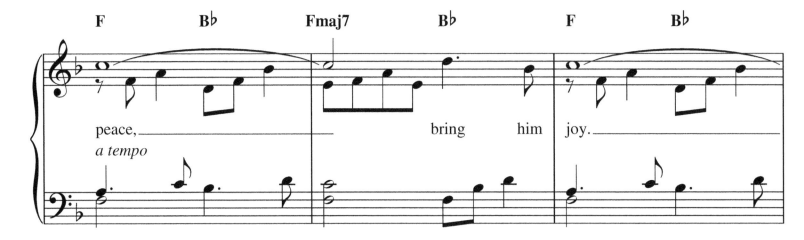

peace,___ *a tempo* bring him joy.___

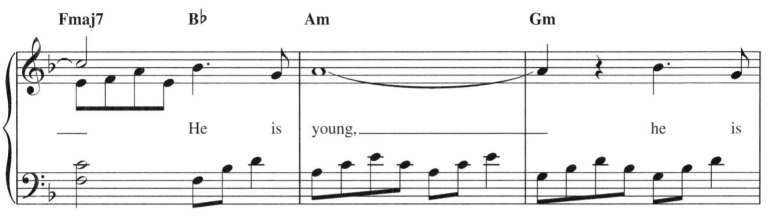

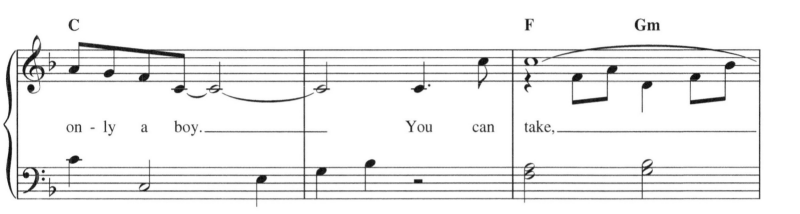

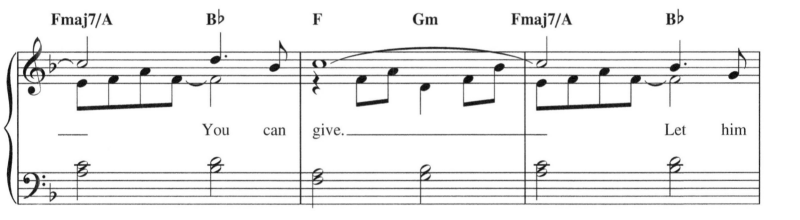

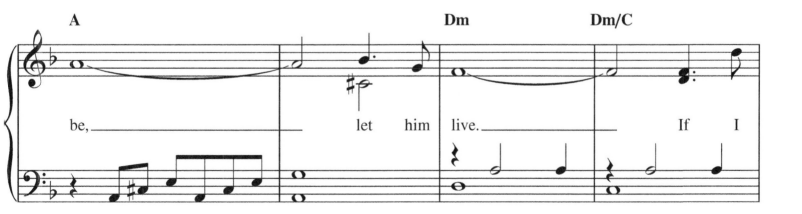

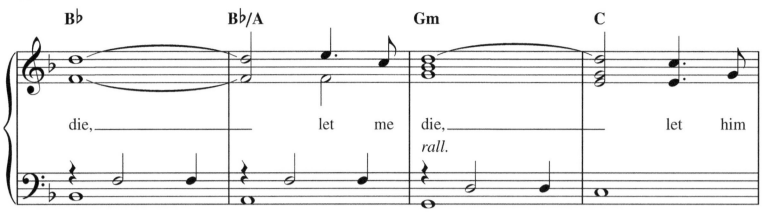

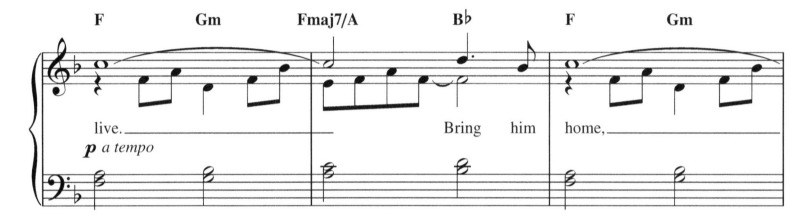

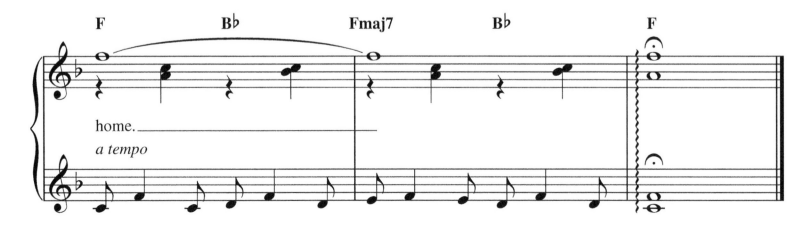

EDELWEISS
from THE SOUND OF MUSIC

Lyrics by OSCAR HAMMERSTEIN II
Music by RICHARD RODGERS

Slowly, with expression

Both hands one octave higher

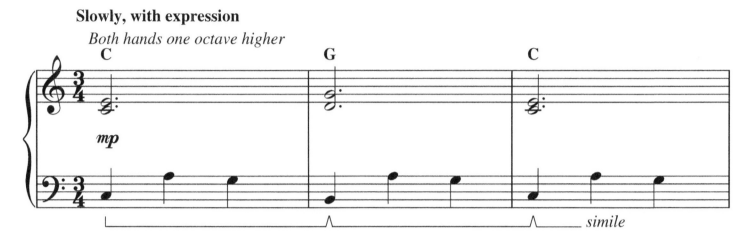

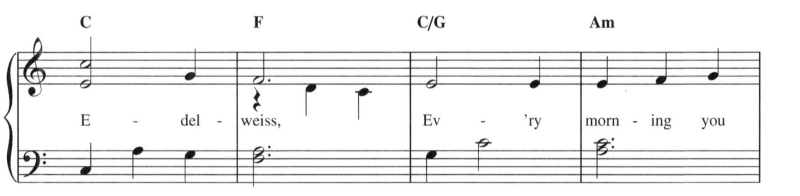

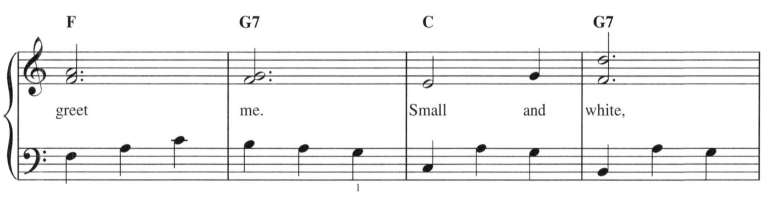

1

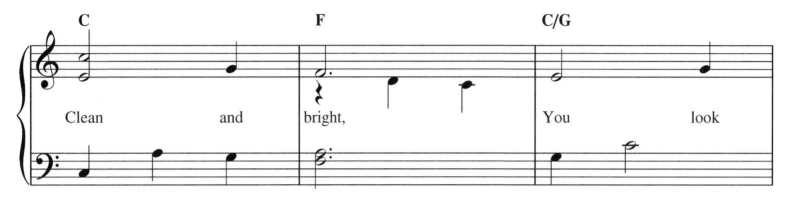

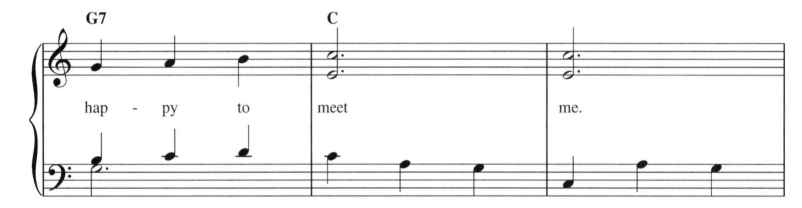

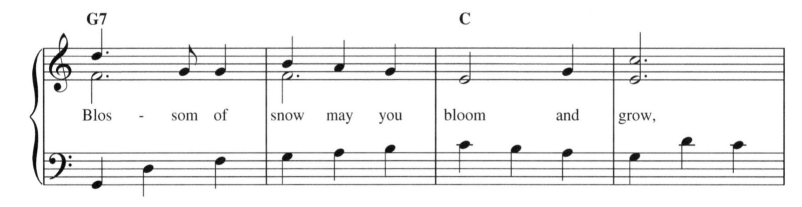

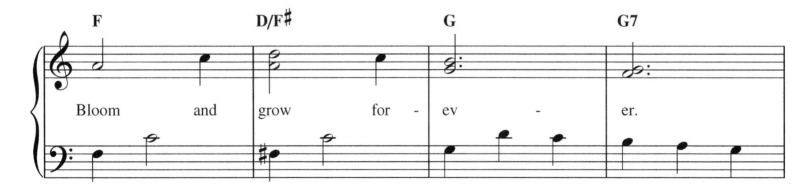

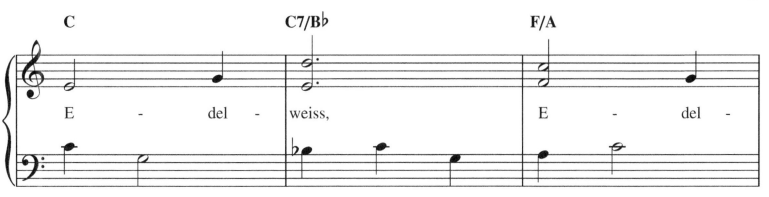

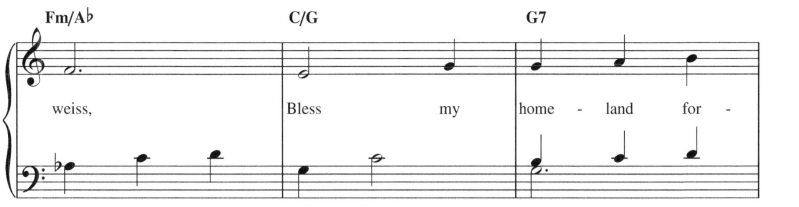

Both hands 8va to end

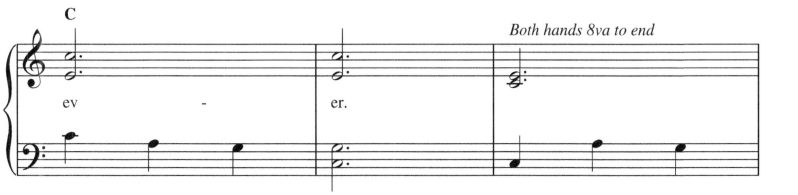

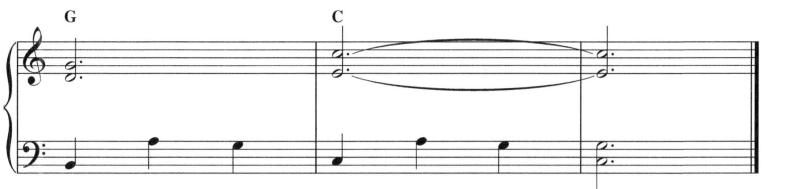

CAN'T HELP LOVIN' DAT MAN

from SHOW BOAT

Lyrics by OSCAR HAMMERSTEIN II
Music by JEROME KERN

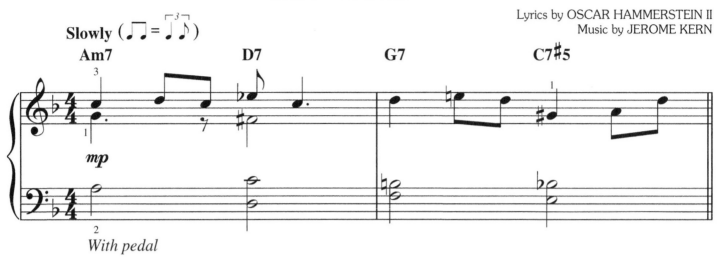

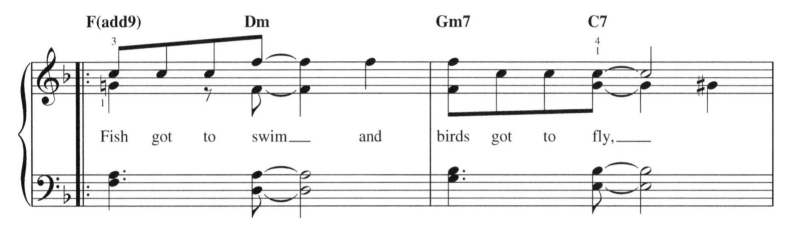

Fish got to swim___ and birds got to fly,___

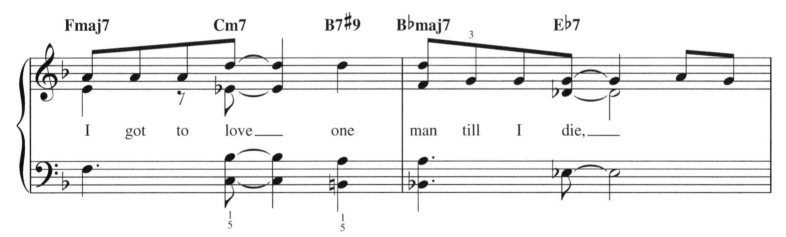

I got to love___ one man till I die,___

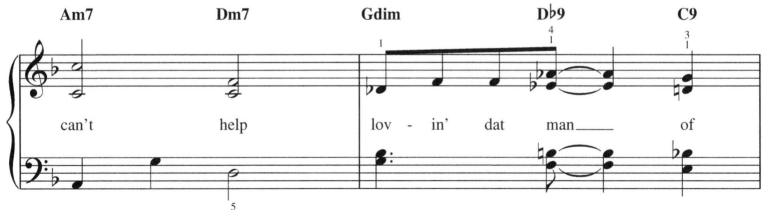

can't help lov-in' dat man___ of

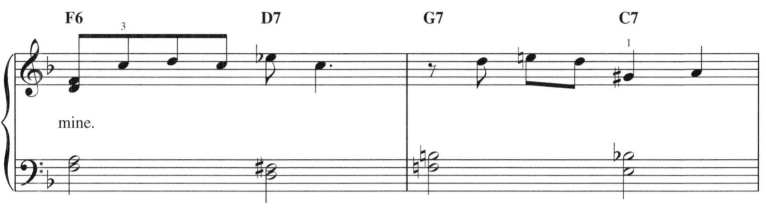

mine.

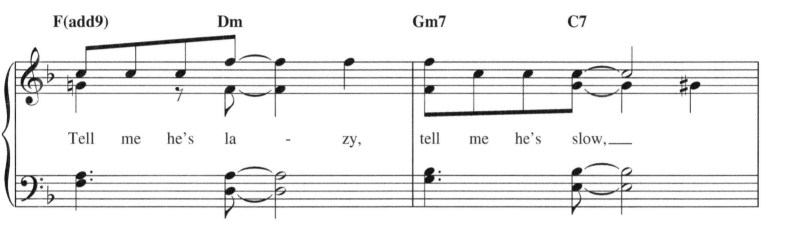

Tell me he's la - zy, tell me he's slow,___

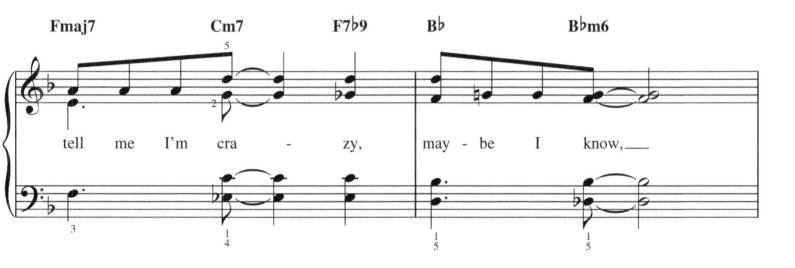

tell me I'm cra - zy, may - be I know,___

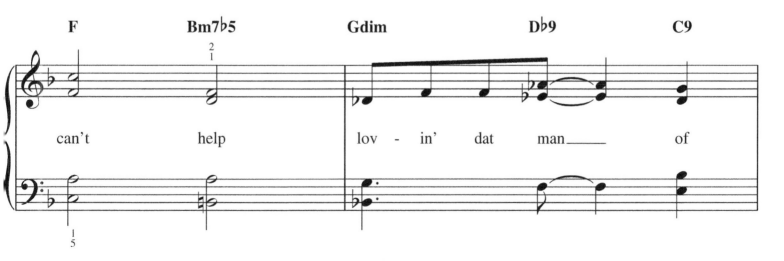

can't help lov - in' dat man___ of

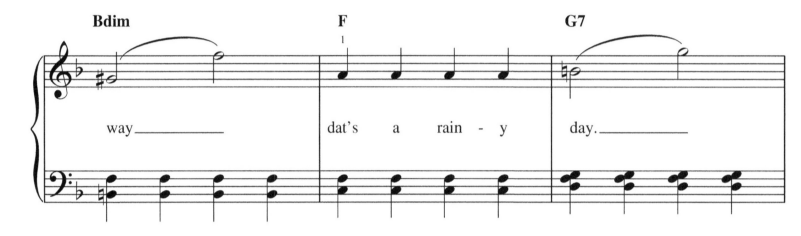

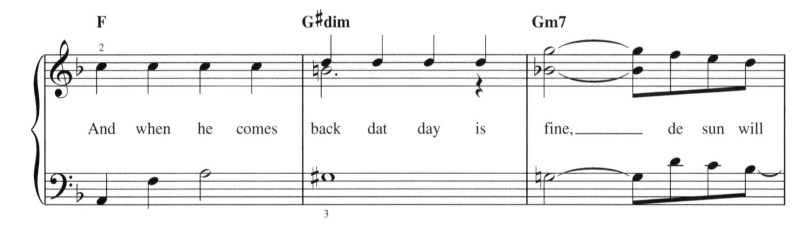

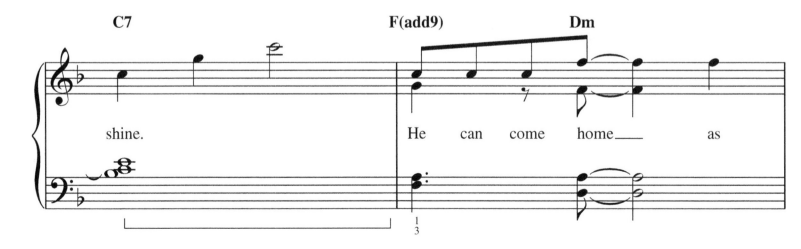

late as can be,_____ home with-out him_____ ain't

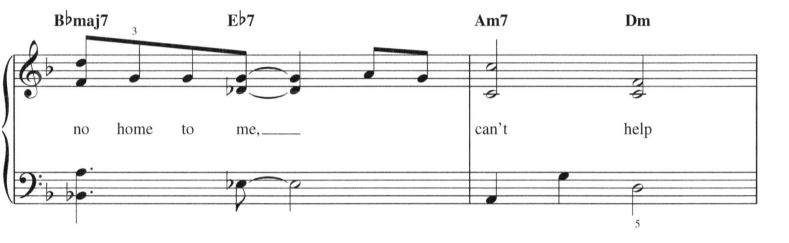

no home to me,_____ can't help

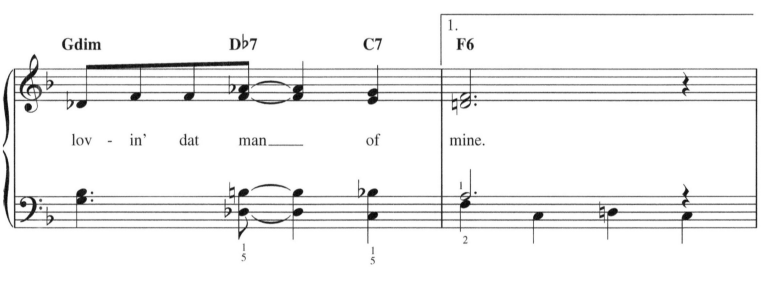

lov - in' dat man_____ of mine.

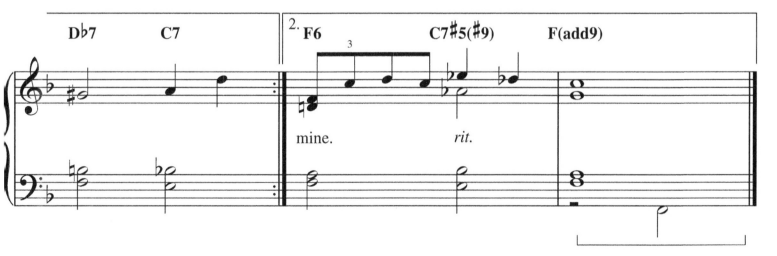

mine. *rit.*

IF EVER I WOULD LEAVE YOU

from CAMELOT

Words by ALAN JAY LERNER
Music by FREDERICK LOEWE

Moderately fast

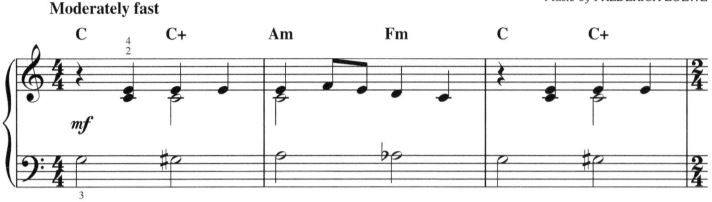

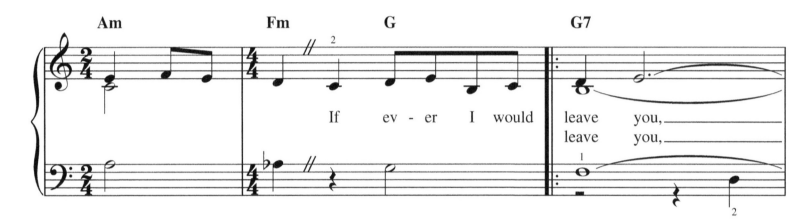

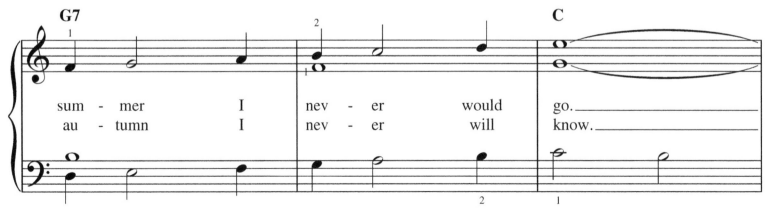

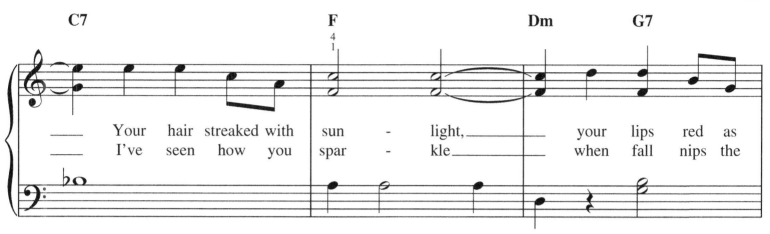

Your hair streaked with sun - light, your lips red as
I've seen how you spar - kle when fall nips the

flame, your face with a lus - ter
air, I know you in au - tumn

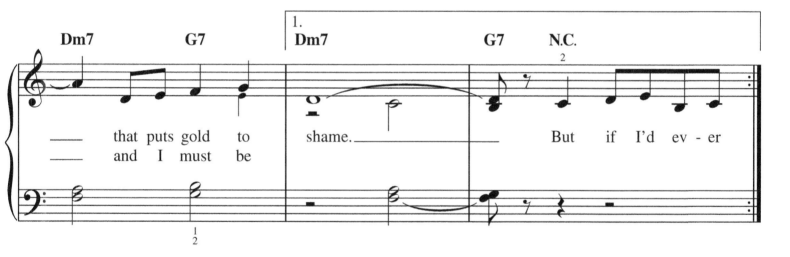

that puts gold to shame. But if I'd ev - er
and I must be

C   Fm/C   C

there. And could I

Rather freely

E   E+

leave you run - ning

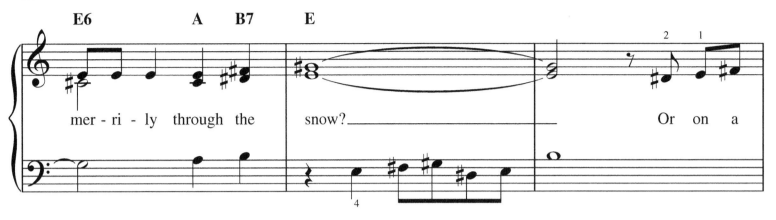

E6   A B7   E

mer - ri - ly through the   snow?   Or on a

G#   C#   G#   F#m7   B7   E

win - t'ry eve - ning   when you catch the fire's   glow?

Again in strict tempo

G7 N.C.   G7

_____ If ev - er I would leave you,_____   how could it be in

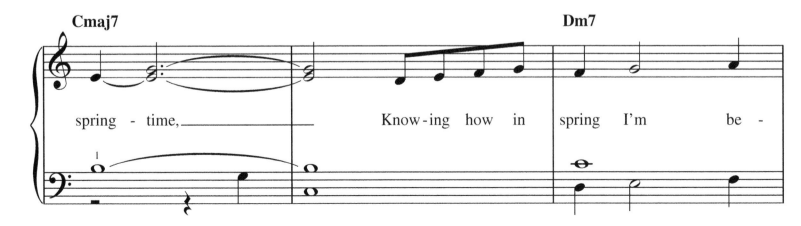

Cmaj7   Dm7

spring - time,_____   Know-ing how in spring I'm be -

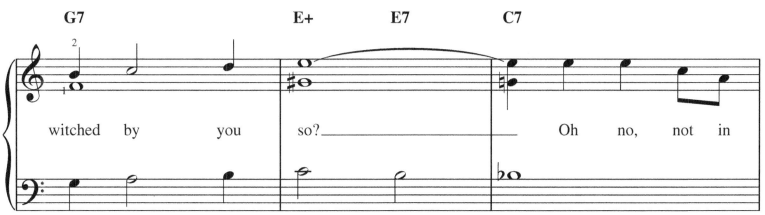

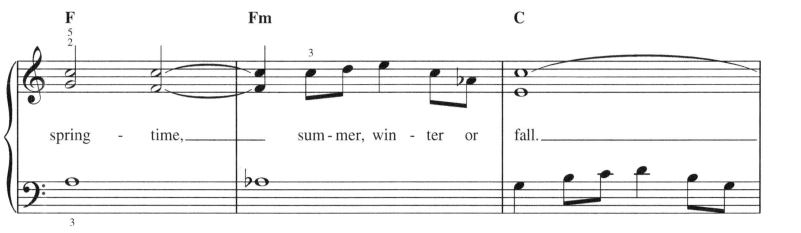

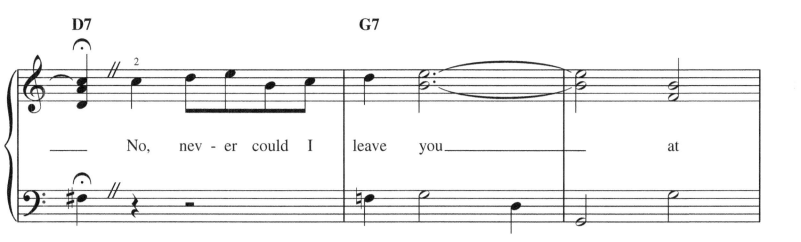

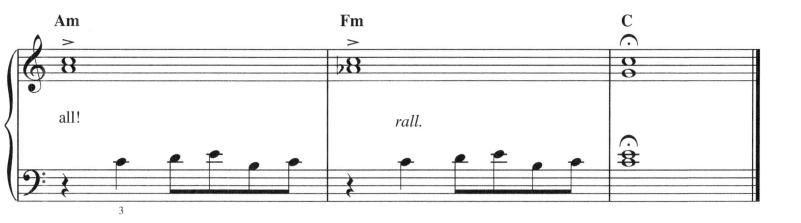

MEMORY
from CATS

Music by ANDREW LLOYD WEBBER
Text by TREVOR NUNN after T.S. ELIOT

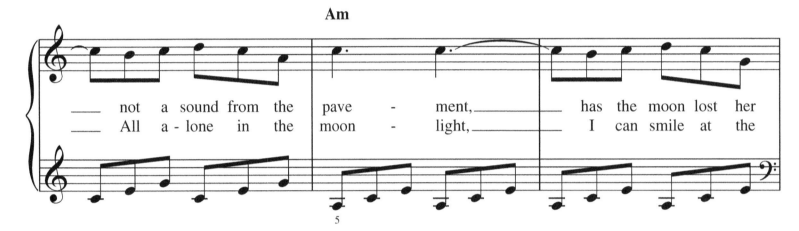

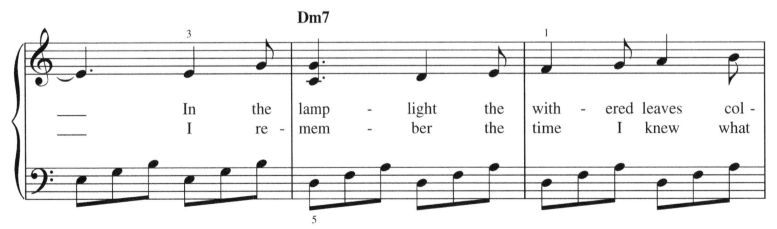

lect at my feet_____ and the wind_____
hap - pi - ness was._____ Let the

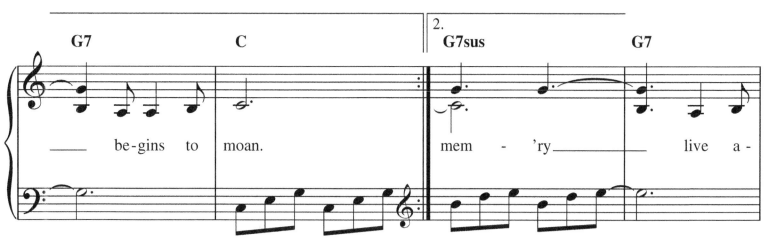

_____ be - gins to moan. mem - 'ry_____ live a -

Faster, in two

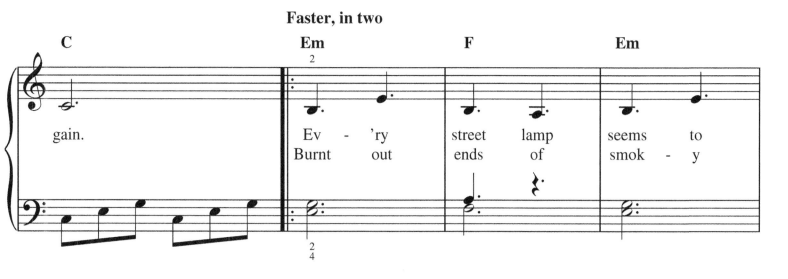

gain. Ev - 'ry street lamp seems to
Burnt out ends of smok - y

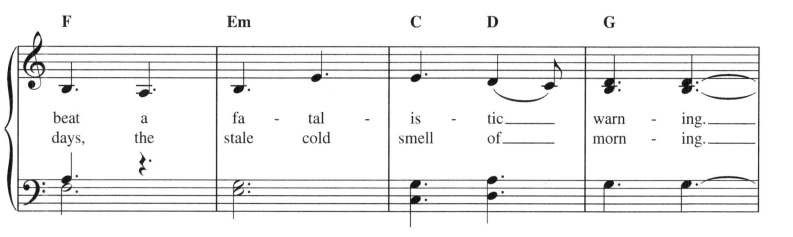

beat a fa - tal - is - tic_____ warn - ing._____
days, the stale cold smell of_____ morn - ing._____

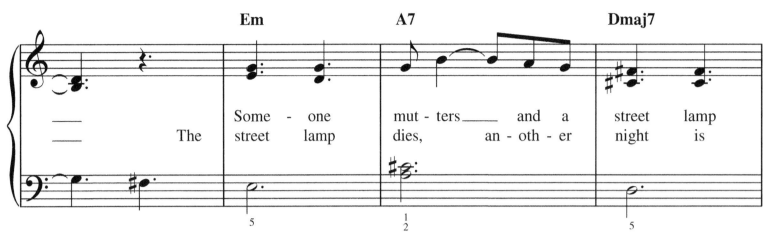

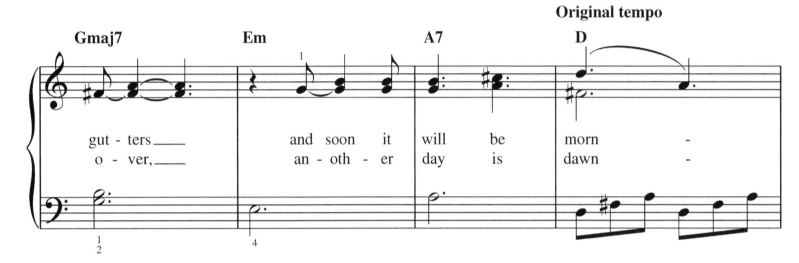

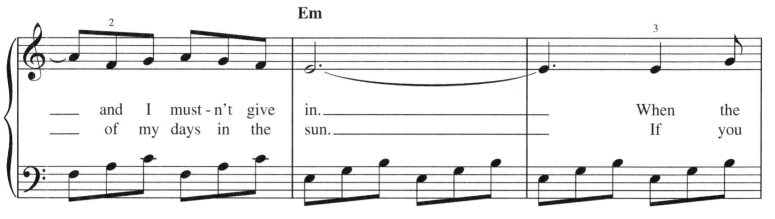

and I must-n't give in._____ When the
of my days in the sun._____ If you

dawn comes to - night will be a mem - o - ry, too,_____
touch me, you'll un - der-stand a what hap - pi - ness is,_____

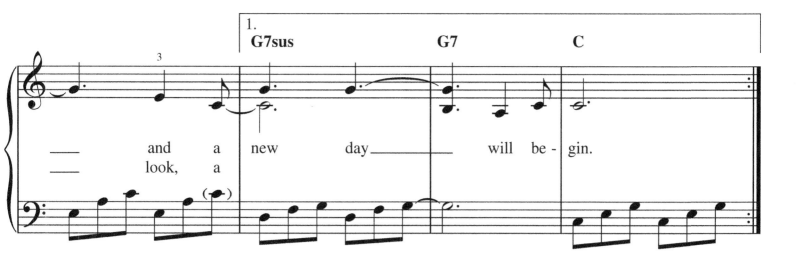

1.

and a new day_____ will be - gin.
look, a

2.

new day_____ has be - gun.

MY FAVORITE THINGS

from THE SOUND OF MUSIC

Lyrics by OSCAR HAMMERSTEIN II
Music by RICHARD RODGERS

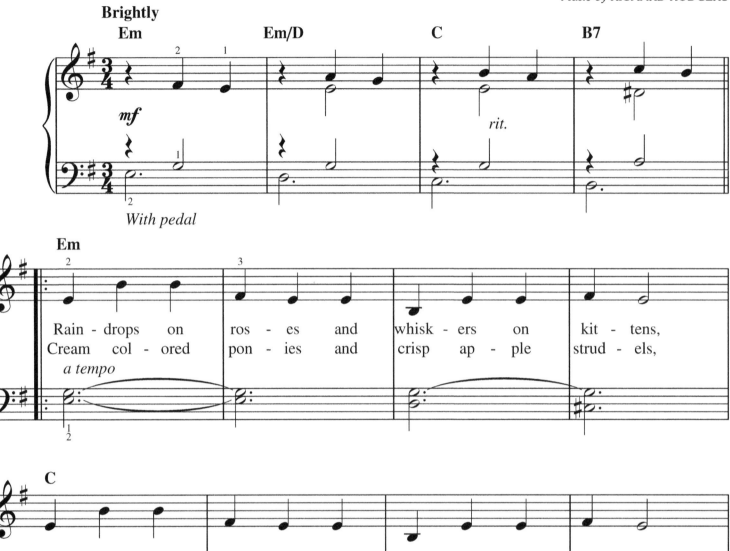

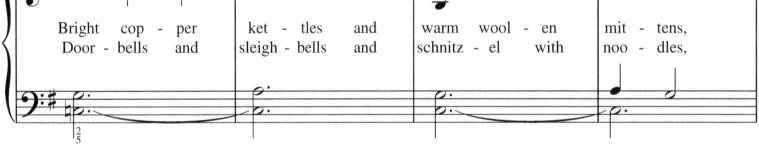

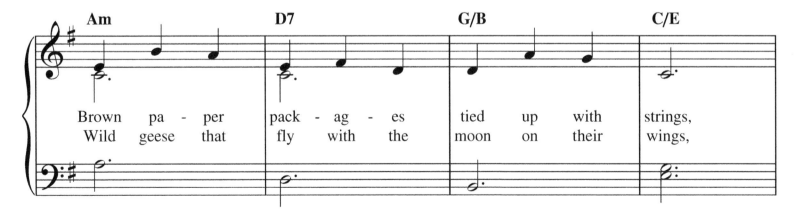

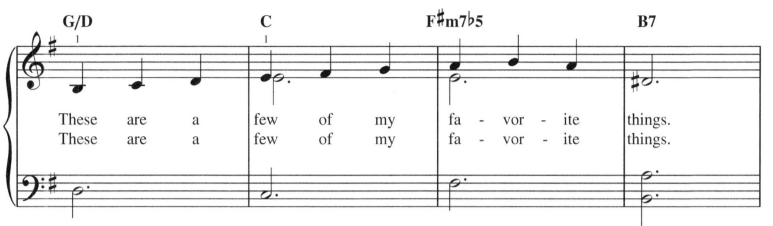

These are a few of my fa - vor - ite things.
These are a few of my fa - vor - ite things.

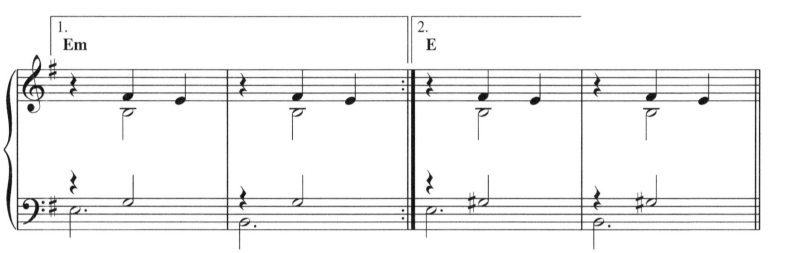

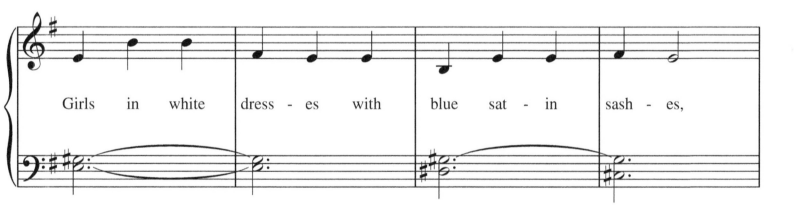

Girls in white dress - es with blue sat - in sash - es,

Snow - flakes that stay on my nose and eye - lash - es,

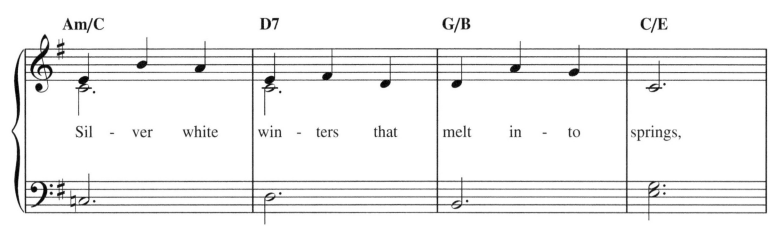

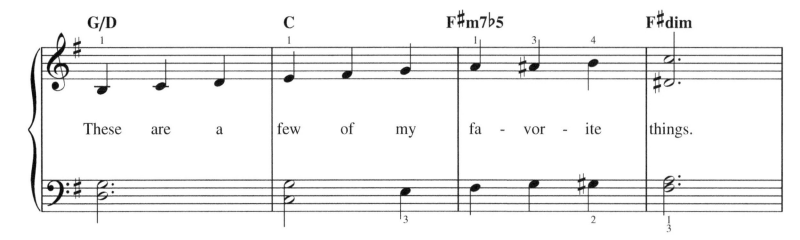

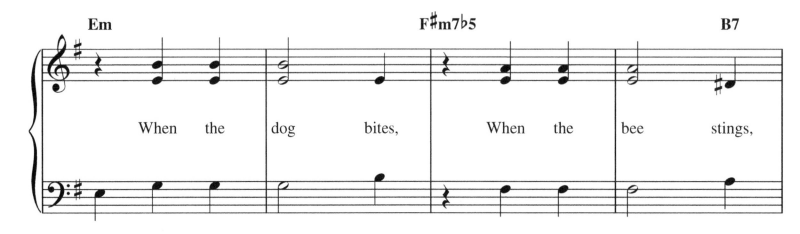

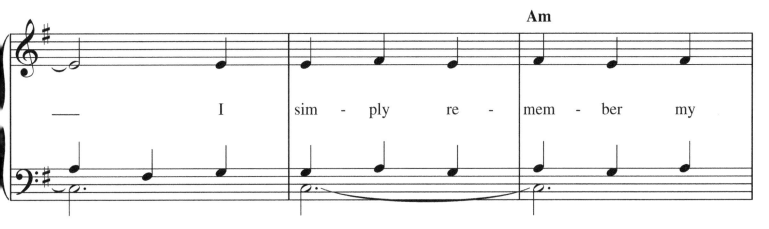

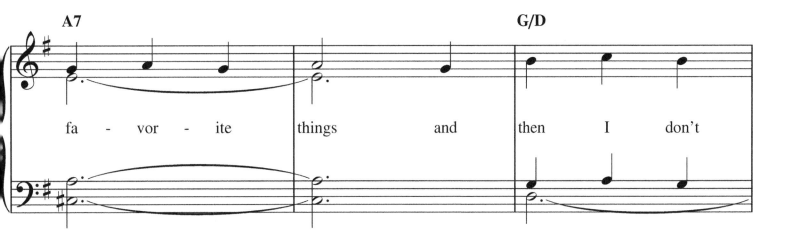

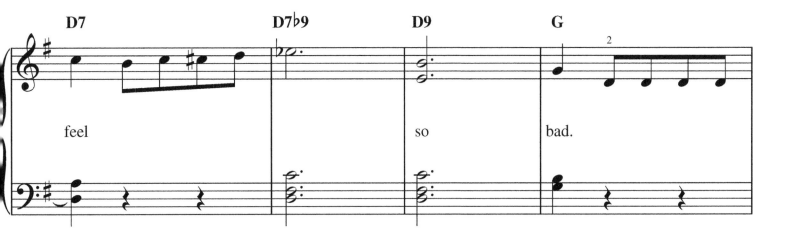

ON A CLEAR DAY
(You Can See Forever)
from ON A CLEAR DAY YOU CAN SEE FOREVER

Words by ALAN JAY LERNER
Music by BURTON LANE

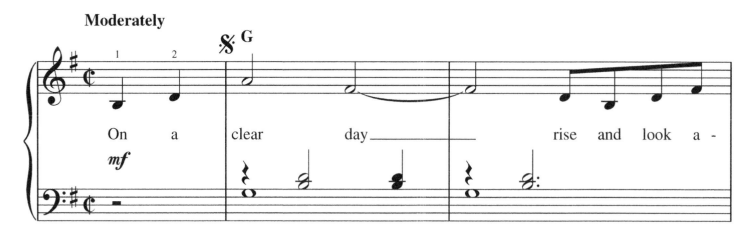

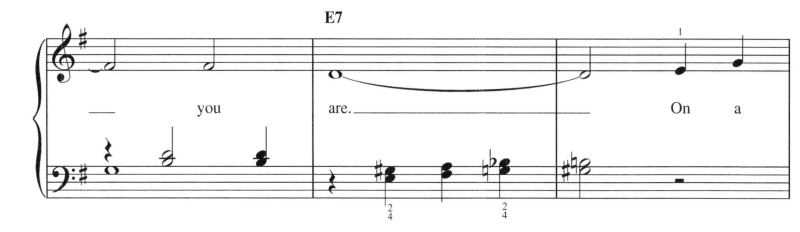

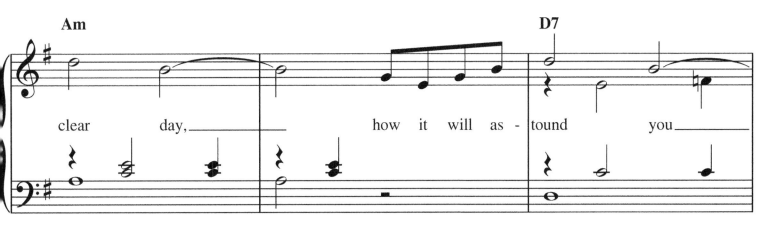

clear day,_____ _____ how it will as - tound you_____

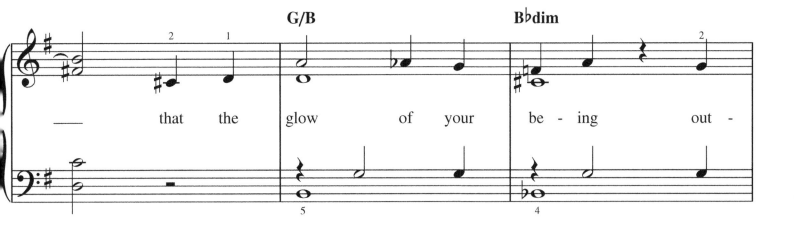

_____ that the glow of your be - ing out -

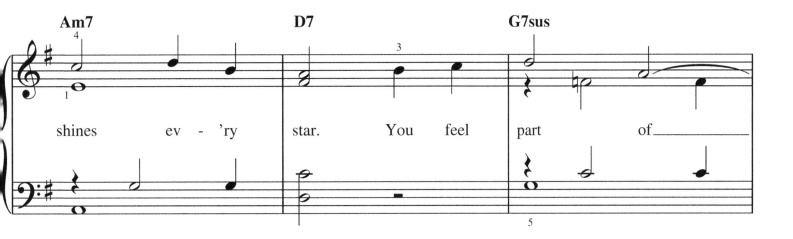

shines ev - 'ry star. You feel part of_____

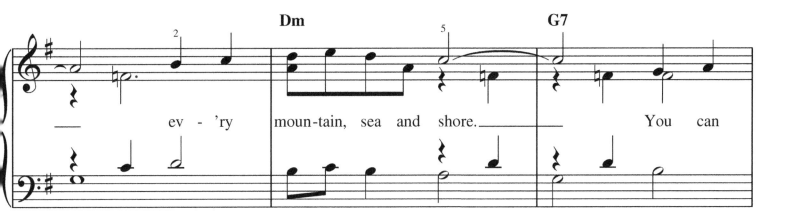

_____ ev - 'ry moun-tain, sea and shore._____ You can

hear, from far and near, a world you've nev - er heard be - fore._____

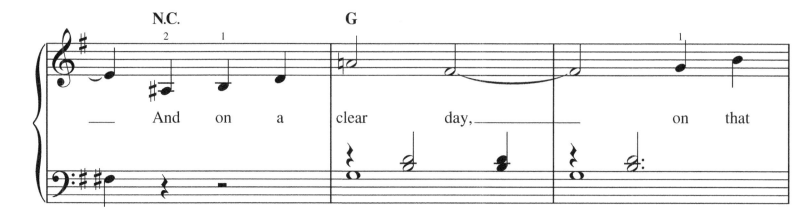

_____ And on a clear day,_____ _____ on that

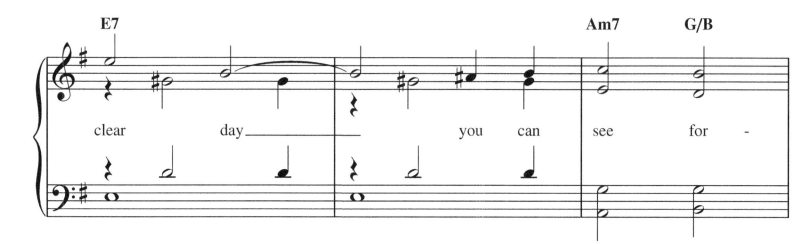

clear day_____ _____ you can see for -

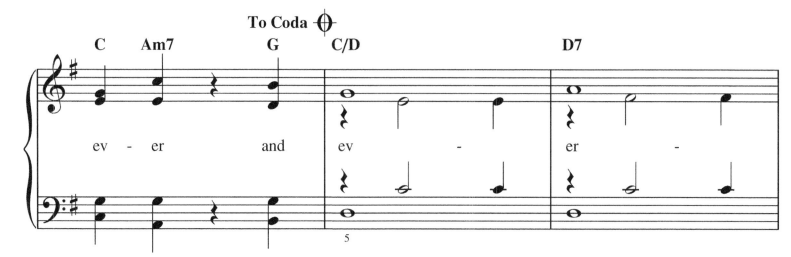

ev - er and ev - er -

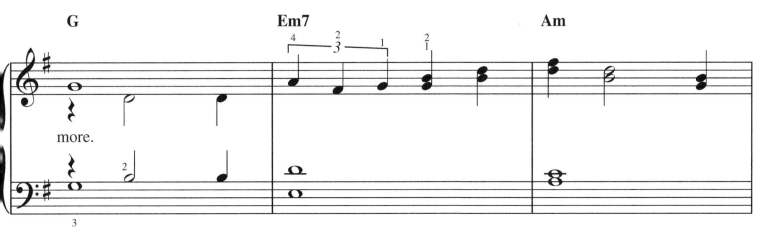

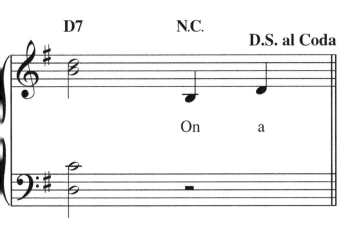
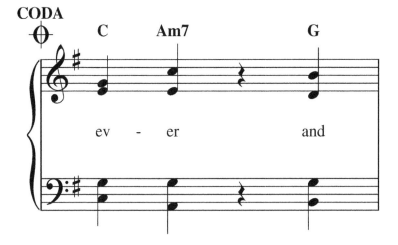

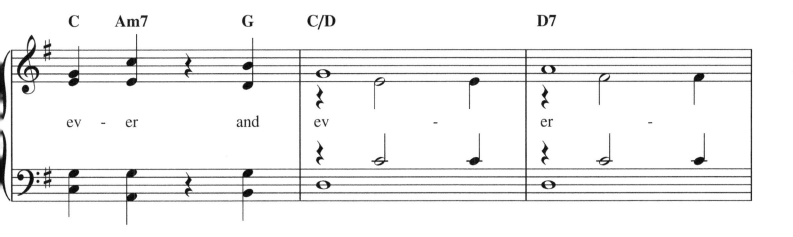

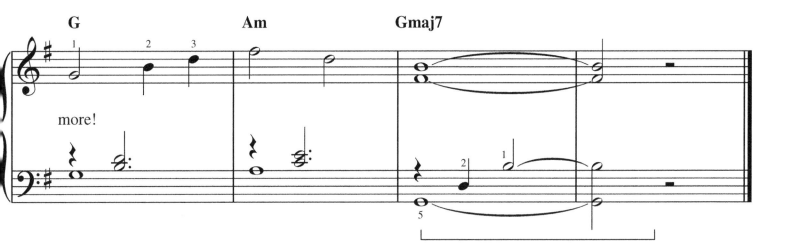

ON THE STREET WHERE YOU LIVE

from MY FAIR LADY

Words by ALAN JAY LERNER
Music by FREDERICK LOEWE

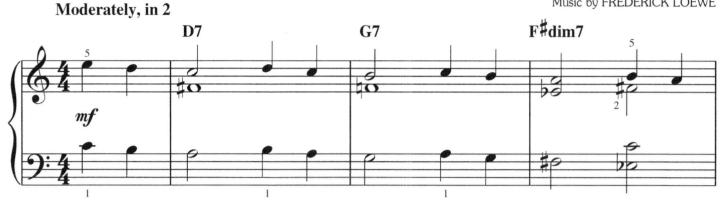

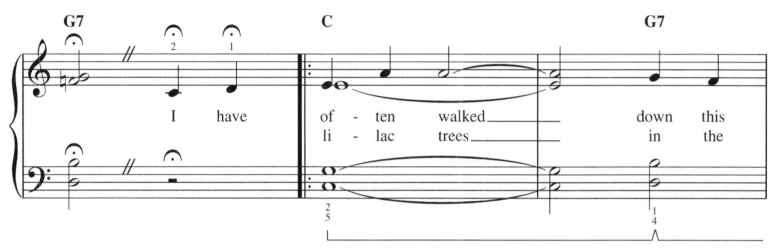

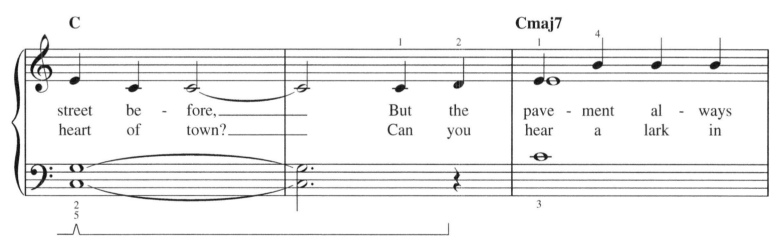

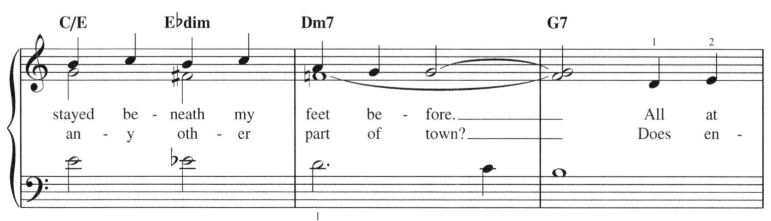

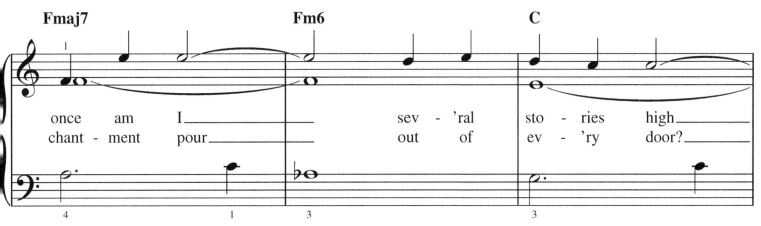

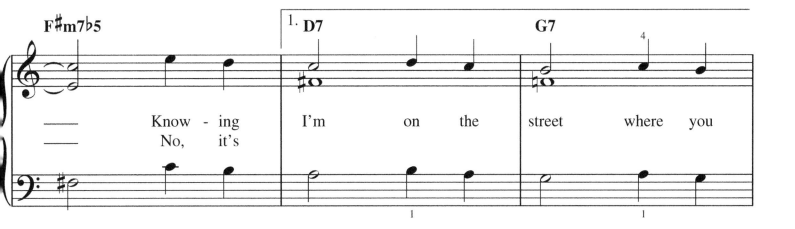

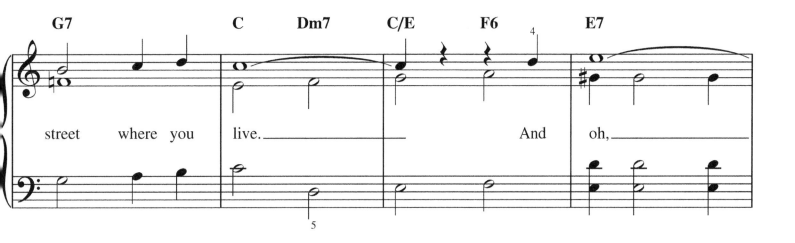

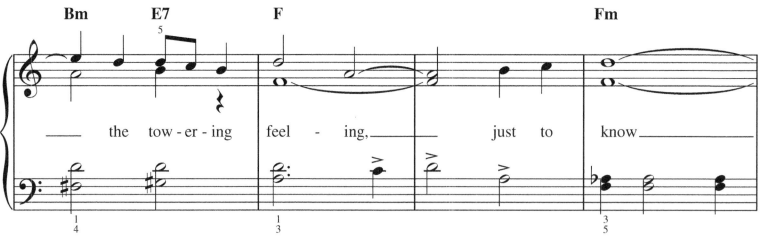

the tow - er - ing feel - ing, just to know

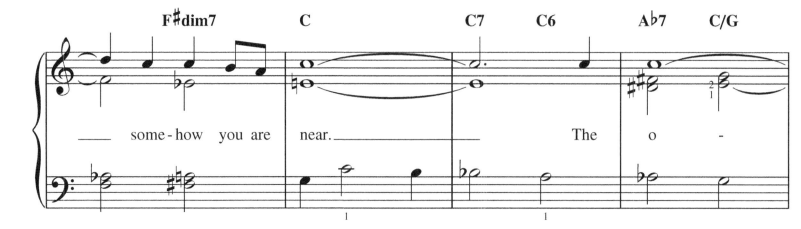

some - how you are near. The o -

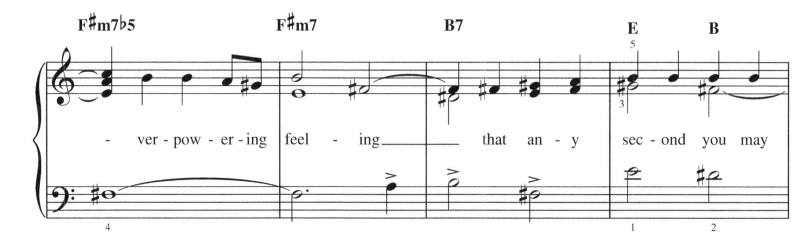

- ver - pow - er - ing feel - ing that an - y sec - ond you may

sud - den - ly ap - pear. Peo - ple stop and stare,

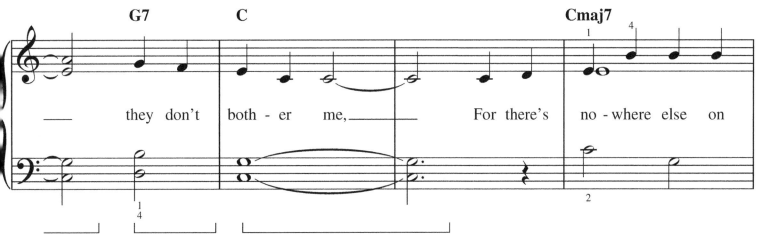

they don't both - er me,_____ For there's no - where else on

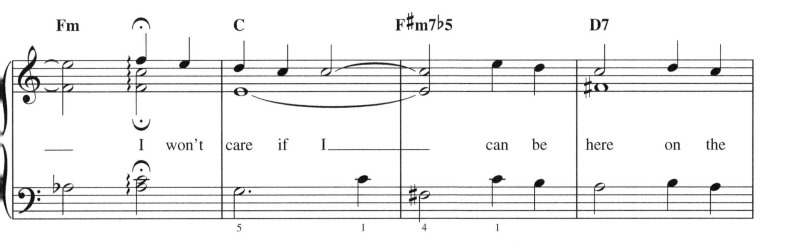

earth that I would rath - er be._____ Let the time go by,_____

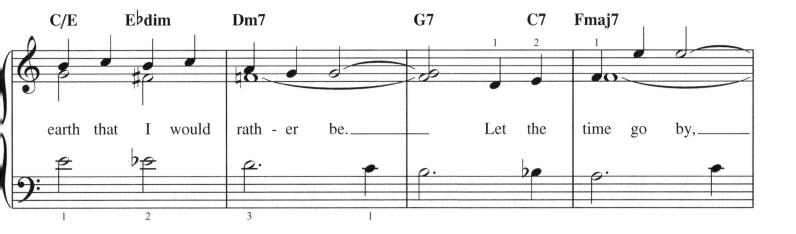

_____ I won't care if I_____ can be here on the

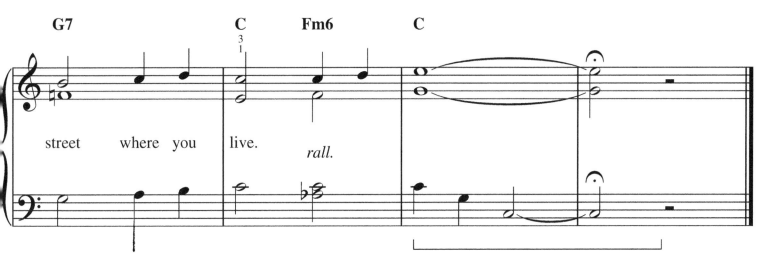

street where you live. *rall.*

SEND IN THE CLOWNS

from the Musical A LITTLE NIGHT MUSIC

Music and Lyrics by
STEPHEN SONDHEIM

Slowly, in one

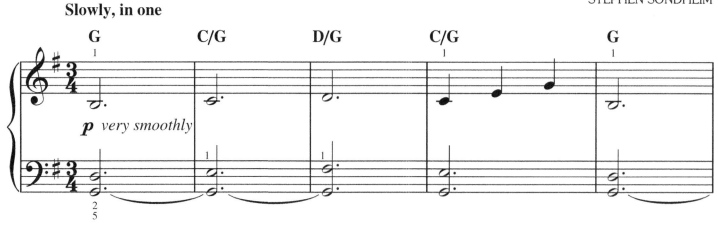

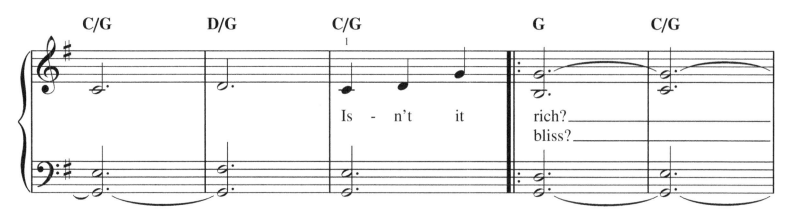

Is - n't it rich?
bliss?

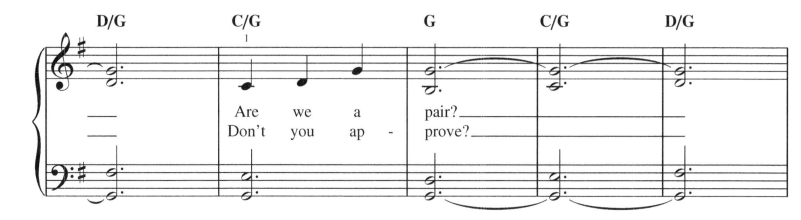

Are we a pair?
Don't you ap - prove?

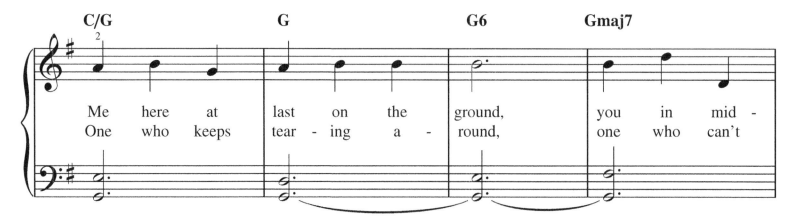

Me here at last on the ground, you in mid -
One who keeps tear - ing a - round, one who can't

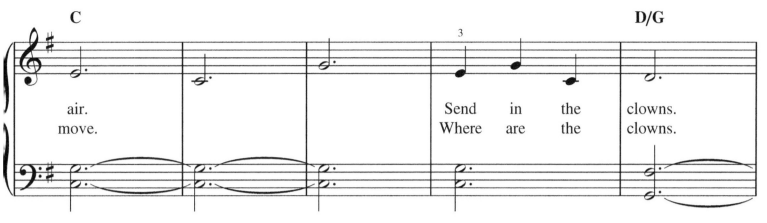

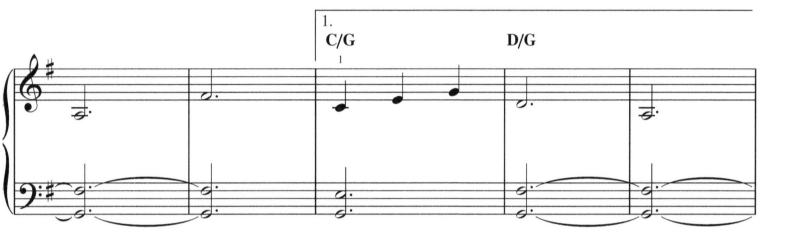

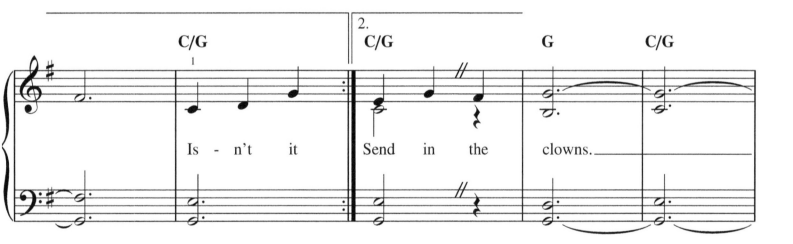

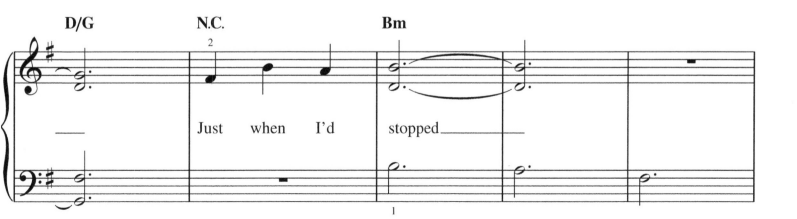

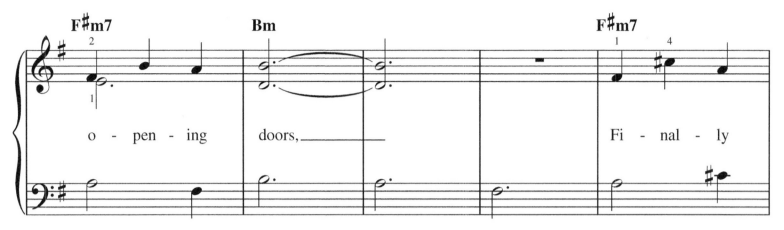

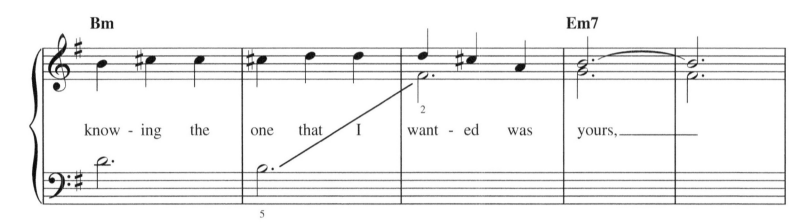

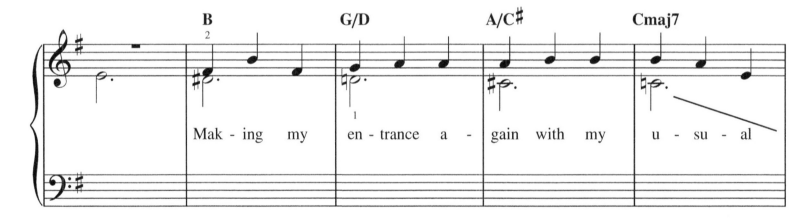

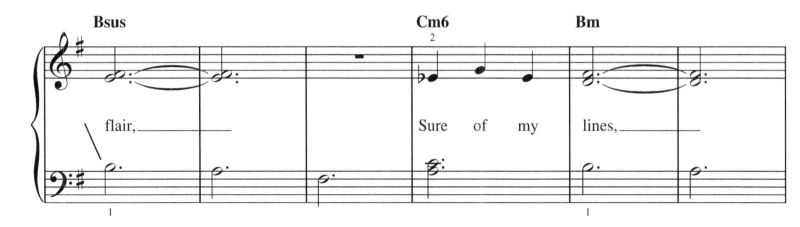

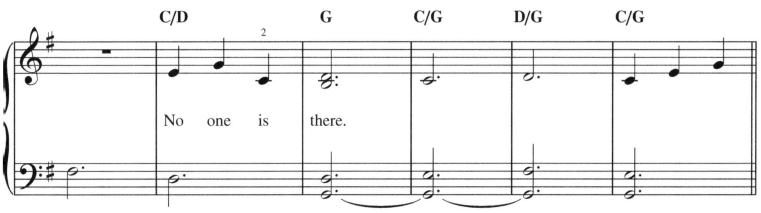

No one is there.

Don't you love farce?_____
Is - n't it rich?_____

My fault I fear,_____
Is - n't it queer?_____

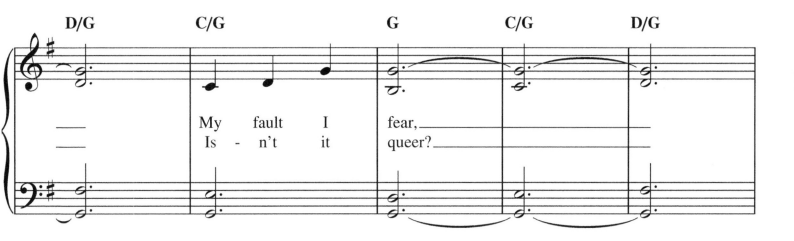

I thought that you'd want what I want. Sor - ry, my
Los - ing my tim - ing this late in my ca -

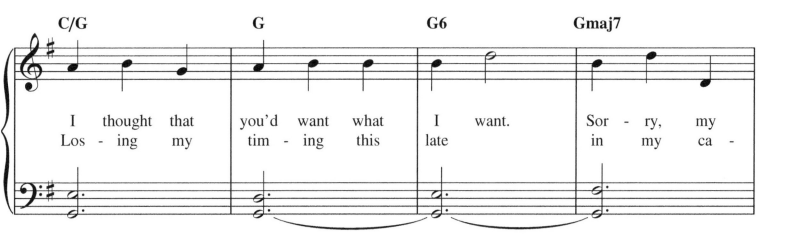

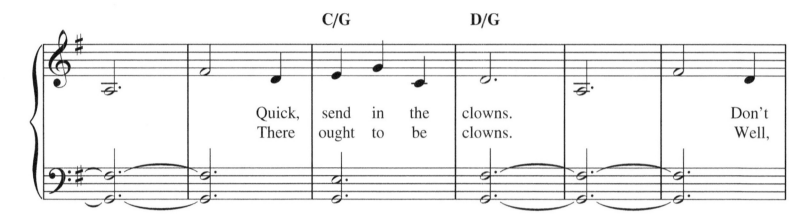

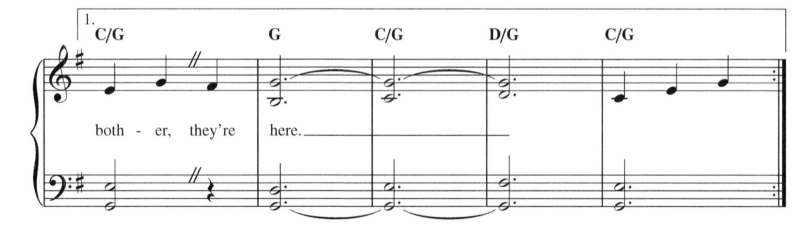

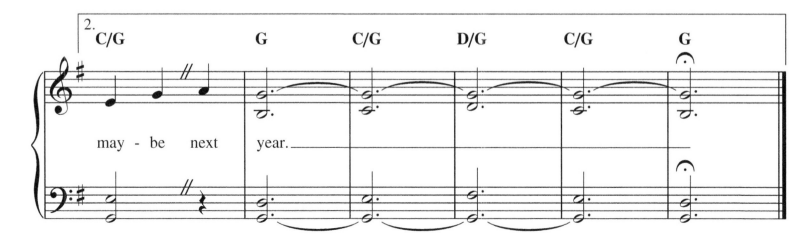

SUMMERTIME
from PORGY AND BESS®

Words and Music by GEORGE GERSHWIN,
DU BOSE and DOROTHY HEYWARD
and IRA GERSHWIN

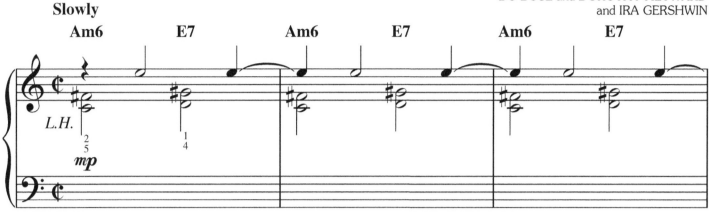

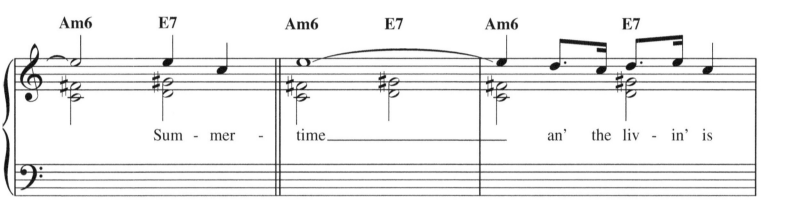

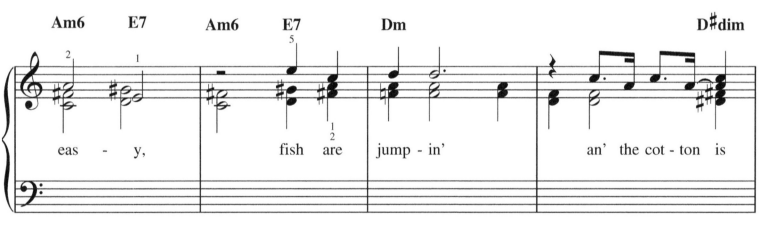

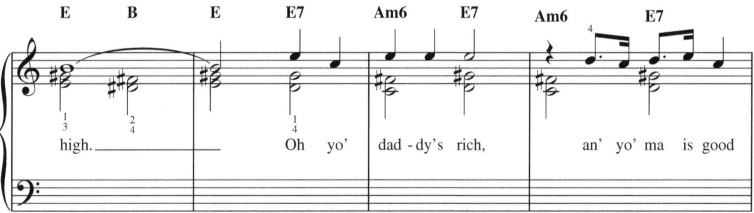

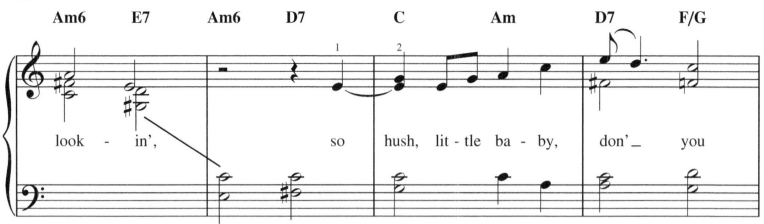

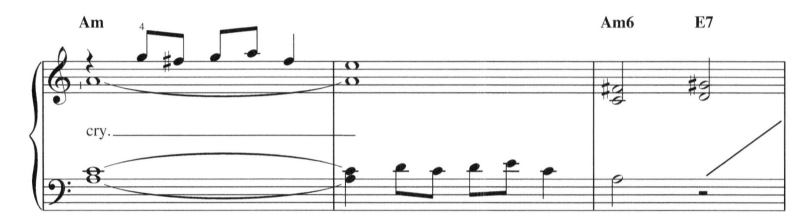

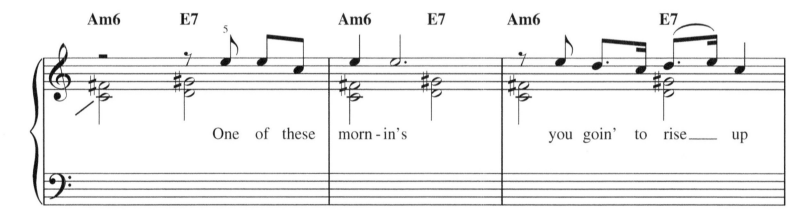

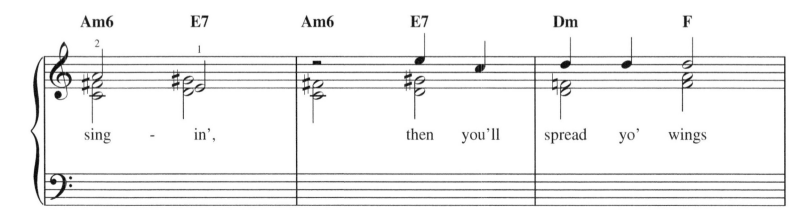

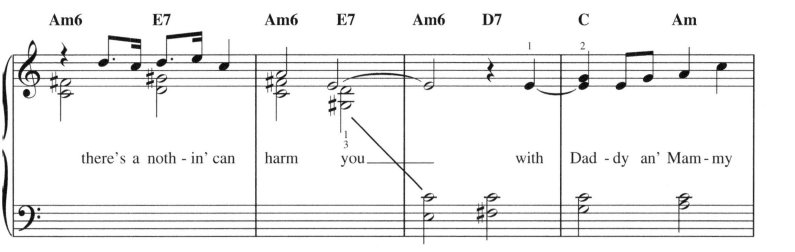

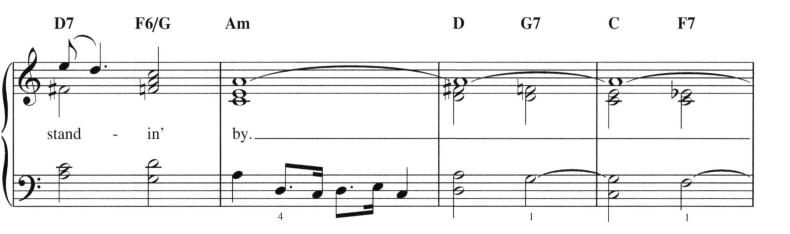

SEPTEMBER SONG
from the Musical Play KNICKERBOCKER HOLIDAY

Words by MAXWELL ANDERSON
Music by KURT WEILL

Moderately

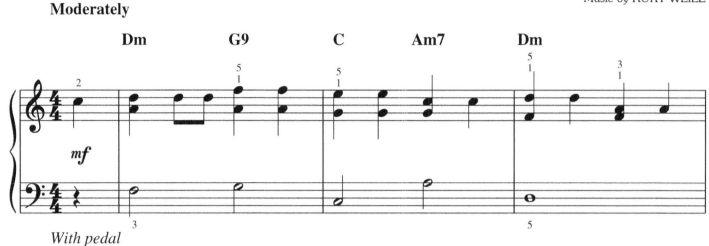

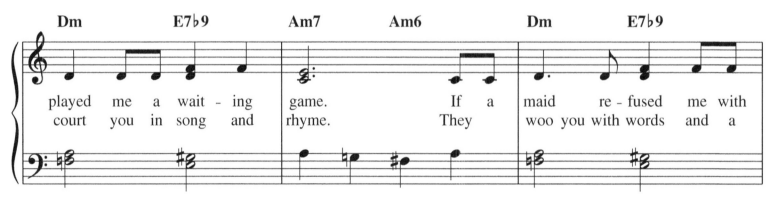

When I was a young man court-ing the girls, I
meet with the young men ear-ly in spring, they

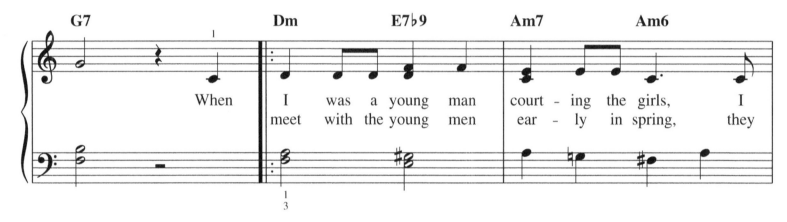

played me a wait-ing game. If a maid re-fused me with
court you in song and rhyme. They woo you with words and a

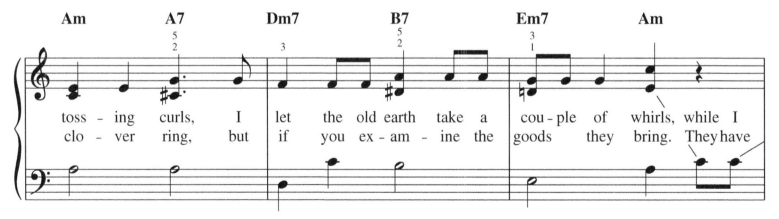

toss-ing curls, I let the old earth take a cou-ple of whirls, while I
clo-ver ring, but if you ex-am-ine the goods they bring. They have

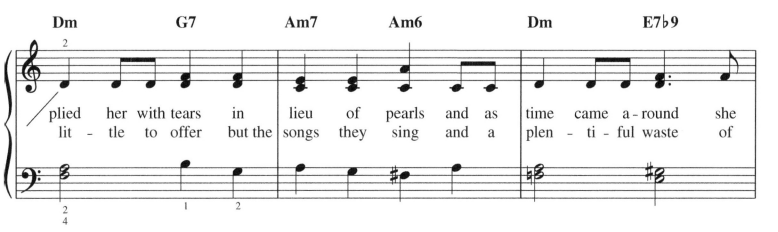

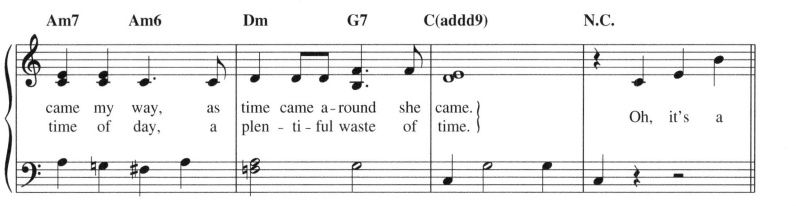

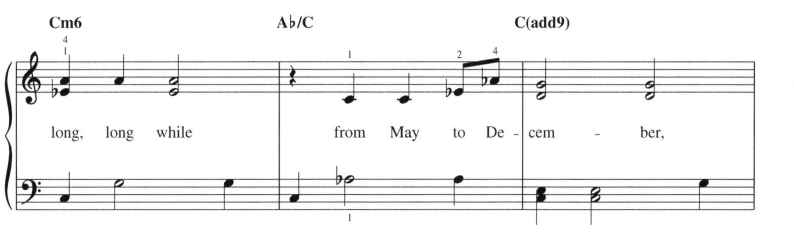

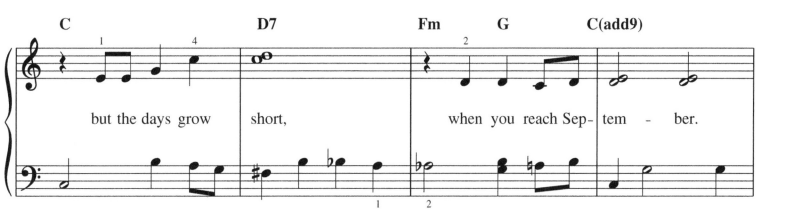

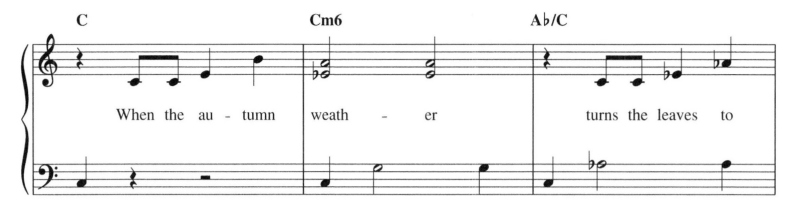

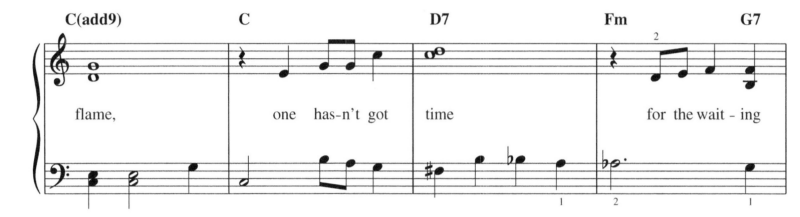

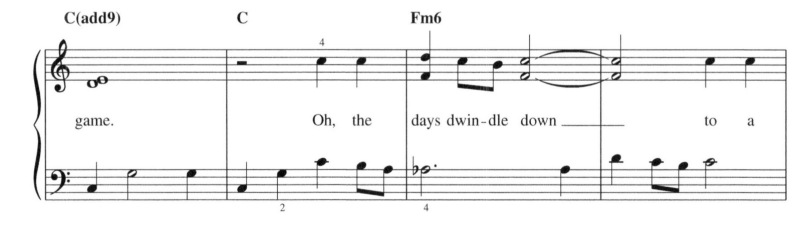

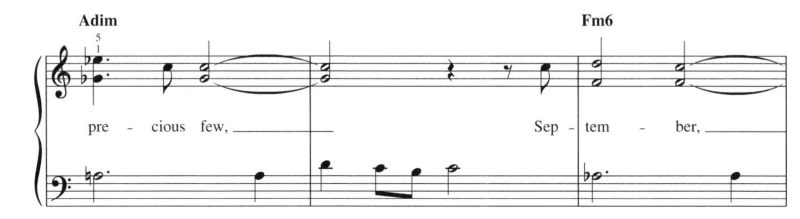

No - vem - ber! And these few

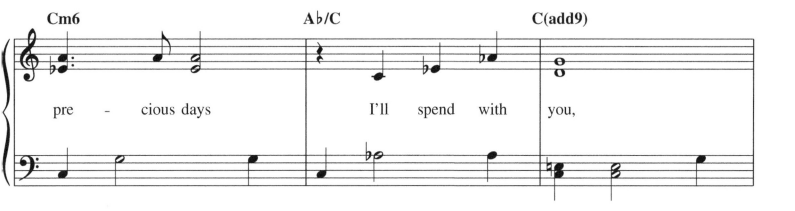

pre - cious days I'll spend with you,

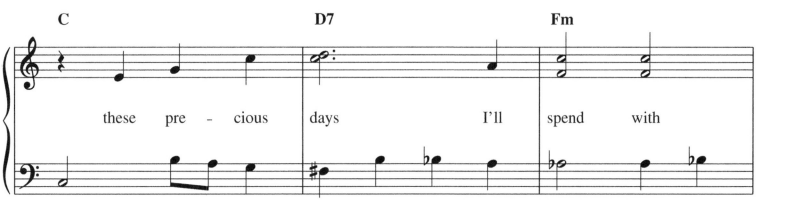

these pre - cious days I'll spend with

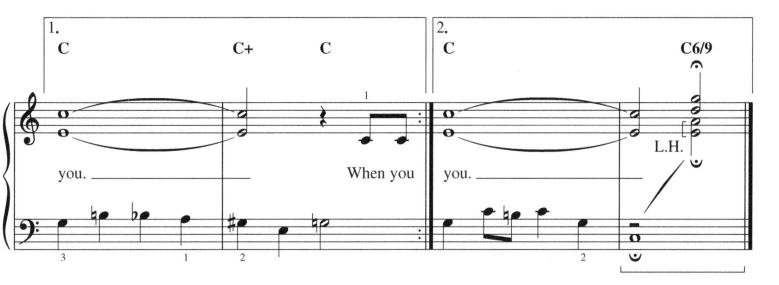

you. _____ When you you. _____

SOME ENCHANTED EVENING

from SOUTH PACIFIC

Lyrics by OSCAR HAMMERSTEIN II
Music by RICHARD RODGERS

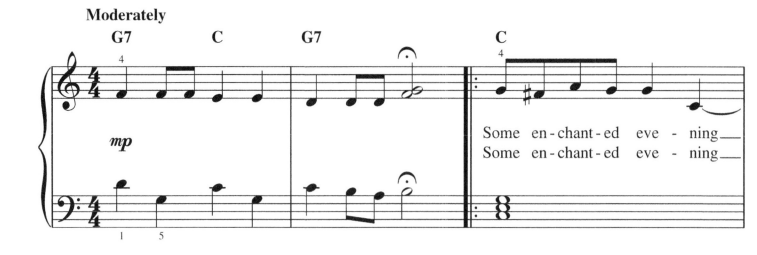

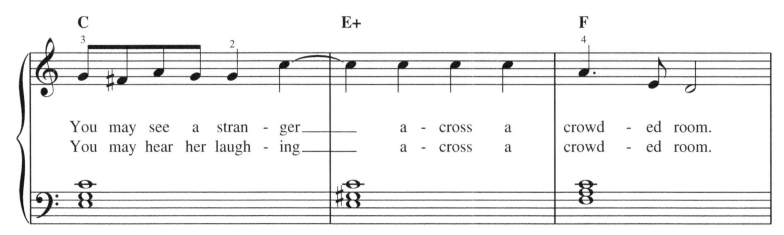

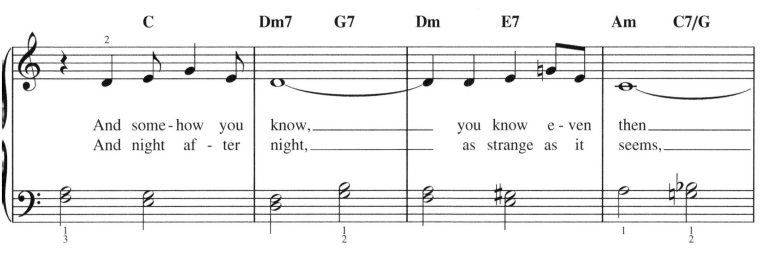

C   Dm7   G7   Dm   E7   Am C7/G

And some-how you know,_____ you know e-ven then_____
And night af - ter night,_____ as strange as it seems,_____

F   C/E   Dm   G

____ that some - where you'll see her a - gain and a -
____ the sound of her laugh - ter will sing in your

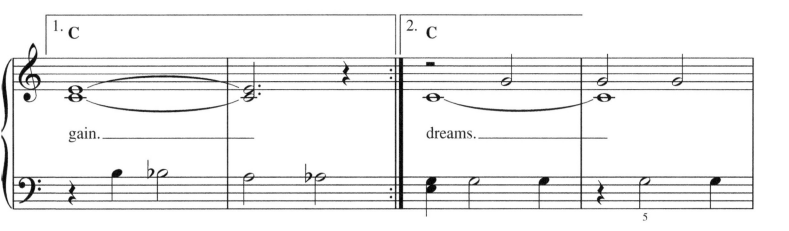

1. C   2. C

gain._____

dreams._____

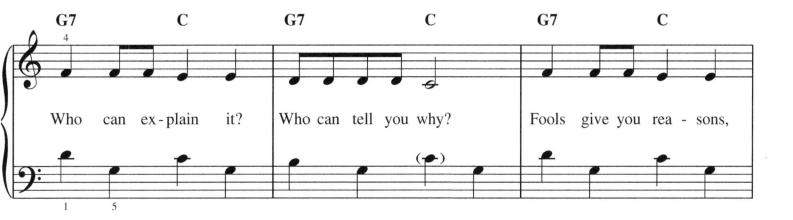

G7   C   G7   C   G7   C

Who can ex-plain it? Who can tell you why? Fools give you rea - sons,

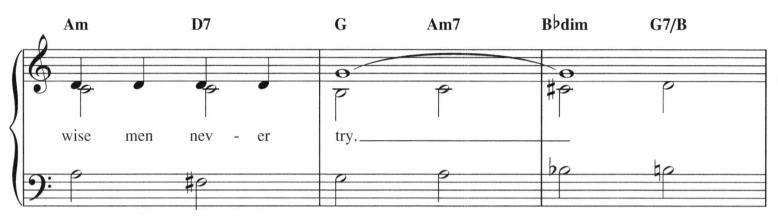

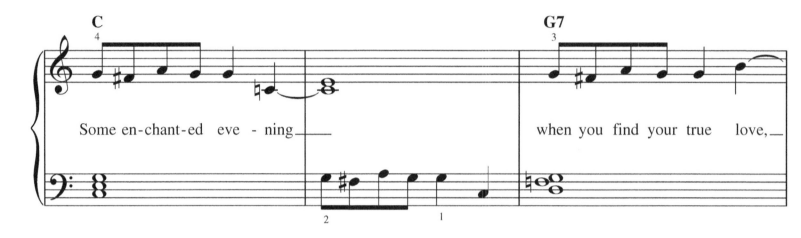

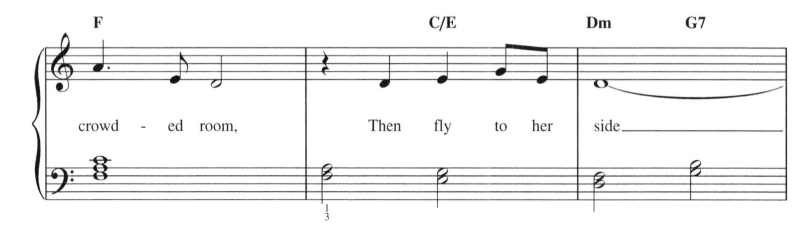

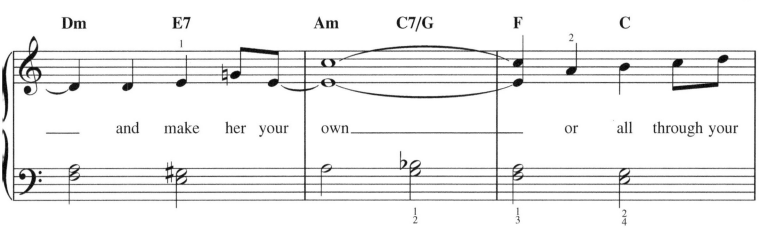

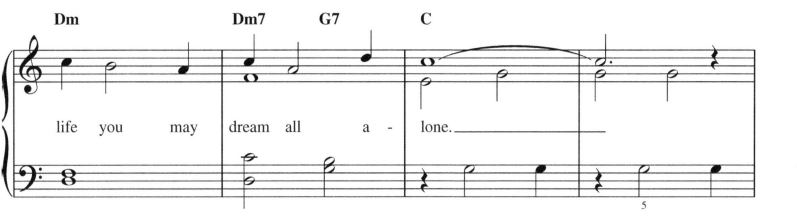

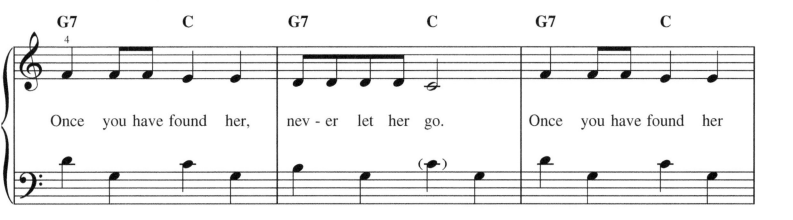

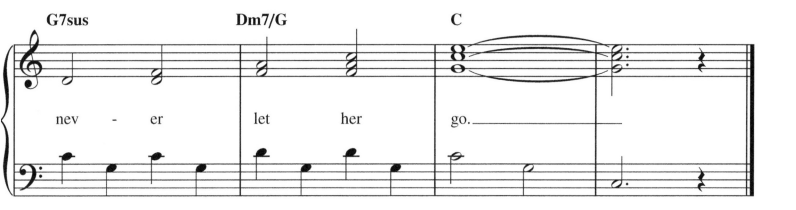

SUNRISE, SUNSET

from the Musical FIDDLER ON THE ROOF

Lyrics by SHELDON HARNICK
Music by JERRY BOCK

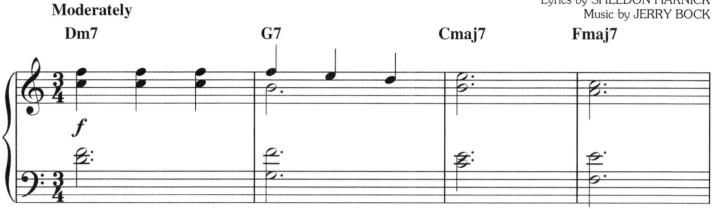

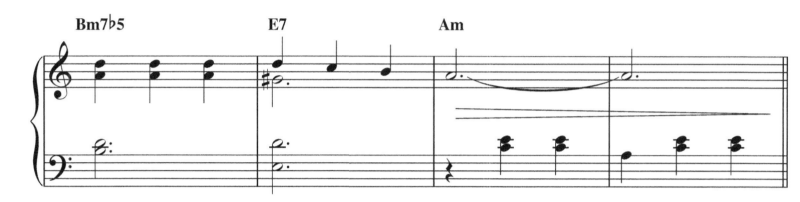

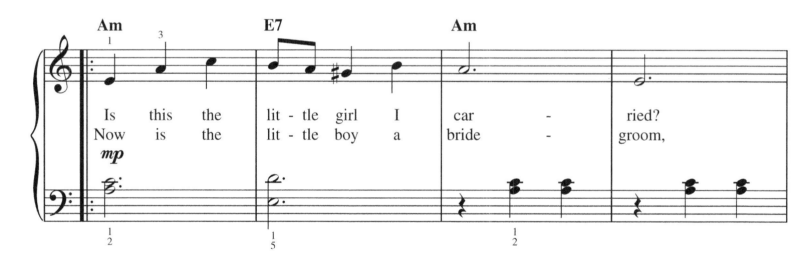

Is this the lit-tle girl I car - ried?
Now is the lit-tle boy a bride - groom,

Is this the lit-tle boy at play?
now is the lit-tle girl a bride.

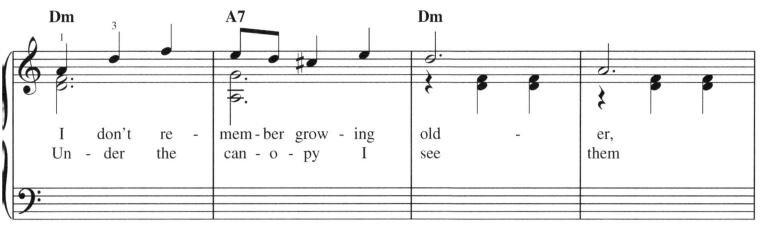

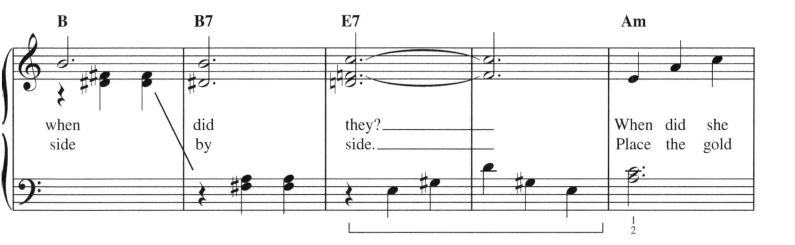

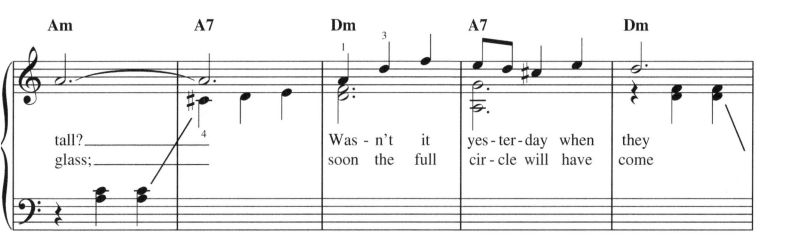

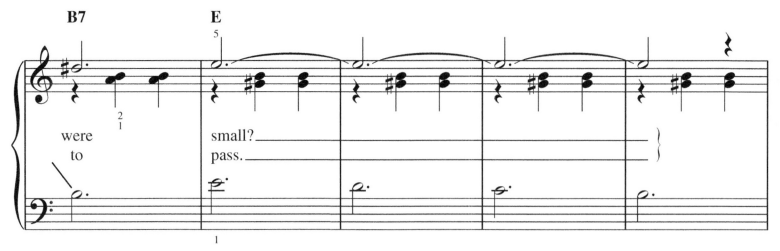

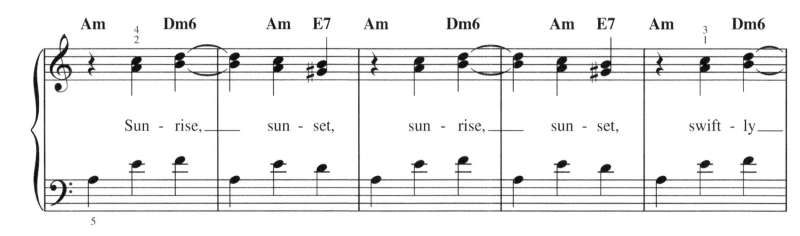

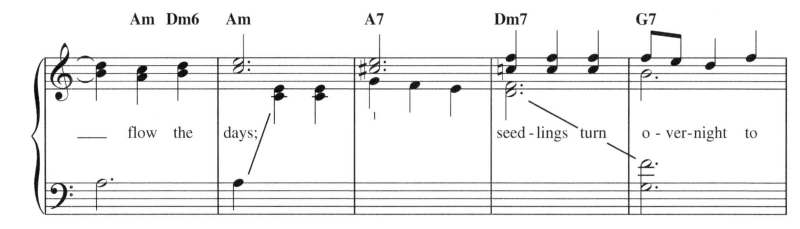

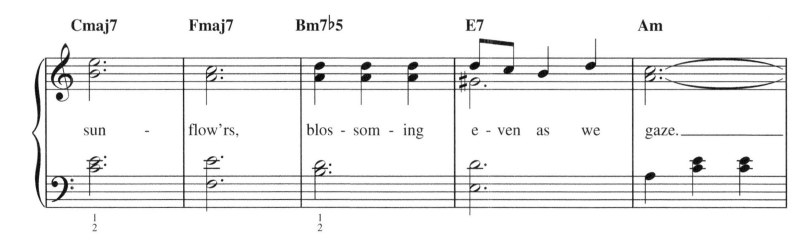

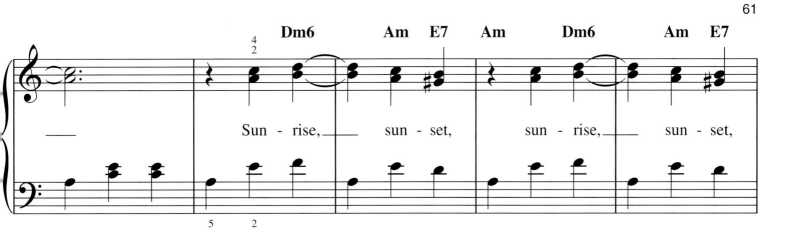

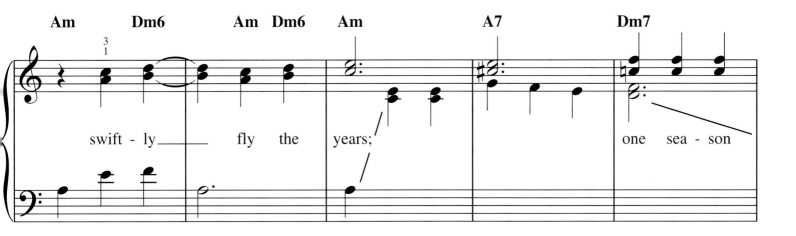

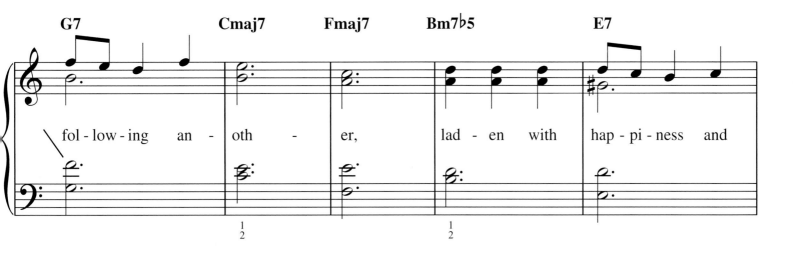

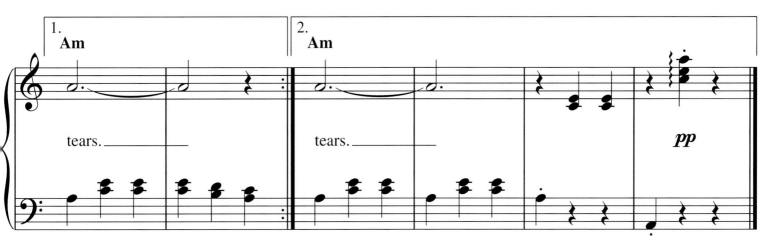

It's Easy to Play Your Favorite Songs with Hal Leonard Easy Piano Books

The Best Praise & Worship Songs Ever

The name says it all: over 70 of the best P&W songs today. Titles include: Awesome God • Blessed Be Your Name • Come, Now Is the Time to Worship • Days of Elijah • Here I Am to Worship • Open the Eyes of My Heart • Shout to the Lord • We Fall Down • and more.
00311312 .... $19.99

First 50 Popular Songs You Should Play on the Piano

50 great pop classics for beginning pianists to learn, including: Candle in the Wind • Chopsticks • Don't Know Why • Hallelujah • Happy Birthday to You • Heart and Soul • I Walk the Line • Just the Way You Are • Let It Be • Let It Go • Over the Rainbow • Piano Man • and many more.
00131140 .... $16.99

The Greatest Video Game Music

28 easy piano selections for the music that envelops you as you lose yourself in the world of video games, including: Angry Birds Theme • Assassin's Creed Revelations • Dragonborn (Skyrim Theme) • Elder Scrolls: Oblivion • Minecraft: Sweden • Rage of Sparta from God of War III • and more.
00202545 .... $17.99

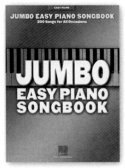

Jumbo Easy Piano Songbook

200 classical favorites, folk songs and jazz standards. Includes: Amazing Grace • Beale Street Blues • Bridal Chorus • Buffalo Gals • Canon in D • Cielito Lindo • Danny Boy • The Entertainer • Für Elise • Greensleeves • Jamaica Farewell • Marianne • Molly Malone • Ode to Joy • Peg O' My Heart • Rockin' Robin • Yankee Doodle • dozens more!
00311014 .... $19.99

Songs from A Star Is Born, The Greatest Showman, La La Land, and More Movie Musicals

Movie musical lovers will delight in this songbook chock full of top-notch songs arranged for easy piano with lyrics from blockbuster movies. Includes: City of Stars from *La La Land* • Suddenly from *Les Misérables* • This Is Me from *The Greatest Showman* • Shallow from *A Star Is Born* • and more.
00287577 .... $17.99

50 Easy Classical Themes

Easy arrangements of 50 classical tunes representing more than 30 composers, including: Bach, Beethoven, Chopin, Debussy, Dvorak, Handel, Haydn, Liszt, Mozart, Mussorgsky, Puccini, Rossini, Schubert, Strauss, Tchaikovsky, Vivaldi, and more.
00311215 .... $14.99

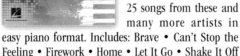
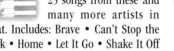

Pop Songs for Kids

Kids from all corners of the world love and sing along to the songs of Taylor Swift, One Direction, Katy Perry, and other pop stars. This collection features 25 songs from these and many more artists in easy piano format. Includes: Brave • Can't Stop the Feeling • Firework • Home • Let It Go • Shake It Off • What Makes You Beautiful • and more.
00221920 .... $14.99

Simple Songs – The Easiest Easy Piano Songs

Play 50 of your favorite songs in the easiest of arrangements! Songs include: Castle on a Cloud • Do-Re-Mi • Happy Birthday to You • Hey Jude • Let It Go • Linus and Lucy • Over the Rainbow • Smile • Star Wars (Main Theme) • Tomorrow • and more.
00142041 .... $14.99

VH1's 100 Greatest Songs of Rock and Roll

The results from the VH1 show that featured the 100 greatest rock and roll songs of all time are here in this awesome collection! Songs include: Born to Run • Good Vibrations • Hey Jude • Hotel California • Imagine • Light My Fire • Like a Rolling Stone • Respect • and more.
00311110 .... $29.99

River Flows in You and Other Eloquent Songs for Easy Piano Solo

24 piano favorites arranged so that even beginning players can sound great. Includes: All of Me • Bella's Lullaby • Cristofori's Dream • Il Postino (The Postman) • Jessica's Theme (Breaking in the Colt) • The John Dunbar Theme • and more.
00137581 .... $14.99

Disney's My First Song Book

16 favorite songs to sing and play. Every page is beautifully illustrated with full-color art from Disney features. Songs include: Beauty and the Beast • Bibbidi-Bobbidi-Boo • Circle of Life • Cruella De Vil • A Dream Is a Wish Your Heart Makes • Hakuna Matata • Under the Sea • Winnie the Pooh • You've Got a Friend in Me • and more.
00310322 .... $17.99

Top Hits of 2019

20 of the year's best are included in this collection arranged for easy piano with lyrics. Includes: Bad Guy (Billie Eilish) • I Don't Care (Ed Sheeran & Justin Bieber) • ME! (Taylor Swift feat. Brendon Urie) • Old Town Road (Remix) (Lil Nas X feat. Billy Ray Cyrus) • Senorita (Shawn Mendes & Camila Cabello) • Someone You Loved (Lewis Capaldi) • and more.
00302273 .... $16.99

HAL•LEONARD®

0320
239

EASY PIANO PLAY-ALONGS
Orchestrated arrangements with you as the soloist!

This series lets you play along with great accompaniments to songs you know and love! Each book comes with recordings of complete professional performances and includes matching custom arrangements in easy piano format. With these books you can: Listen to complete professional performances of each of the songs; Play the easy piano arrangements along with the performances; Sing along with the recordings; Play the easy piano arrangements as solos, without the audio.

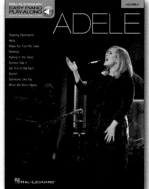

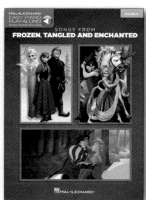

1. GREAT JAZZ STANDARDS
00310916 Book/CD Pack.........................$14.95

2. FAVORITE CLASSICAL THEMES
00310921 Book/CD Pack.........................$14.95

3. BROADWAY FAVORITES
00310915 Book/CD Pack.........................$14.95

4. ADELE
00156223 Book/Online Audio.................$16.99

5. HIT POP/ROCK BALLADS
00310917 Book/CD Pack.........................$14.95

6. LOVE SONG FAVORITES
00310918 Book/CD Pack.........................$14.95

7. O HOLY NIGHT
00310920 Book/CD Pack.........................$14.95

9. COUNTRY BALLADS
00311105 Book/CD Pack.........................$14.95

11. DISNEY BLOCKBUSTERS
00311107 Book/Online Audio.................$14.99

12. CHRISTMAS FAVORITES
00311257 Book/CD Pack.........................$14.95

13. CHILDREN'S SONGS
00311258 Book/CD Pack.........................$14.95

15. DISNEY'S BEST
00311260 Book/Online Audio.................$16.99

16. LENNON & MCCARTNEY HITS
00311262 Book/CD Pack.........................$14.95

17. HOLIDAY HITS
00311329 Book/CD Pack.........................$14.95

18. WEST SIDE STORY
00130739 Book/Online Audio................$14.99

19. TAYLOR SWIFT
00142735 Book/Online Audio................$14.99

20. ANDREW LLOYD WEBBER – FAVORITES
00311775 Book/CD Pack.........................$14.99

21. GREAT CLASSICAL MELODIES
00311776 Book/CD Pack.........................$14.99

22. ANDREW LLOYD WEBBER – HITS
00311785 Book/CD Pack.........................$14.99

23. DISNEY CLASSICS
00311836 Book/CD Pack.........................$14.99

24. LENNON & MCCARTNEY FAVORITES
00311837 Book/CD Pack.........................$14.99

26. WICKED
00311882 Book/CD Pack.........................$16.99

27. THE SOUND OF MUSIC
00311897 Book/Online Audio.................$14.99

28. CHRISTMAS CAROLS
00311912 Book/CD Pack.........................$14.99

29. CHARLIE BROWN CHRISTMAS
00311913 Book/CD Pack.........................$14.99

31. STAR WARS
00110283 Book/Online Audio................$16.99

32. SONGS FROM FROZEN, TANGLED AND ENCHANTED
00126896 Book/Online Audio................$14.99

Disney characters and artwork © Disney Enterprises, Inc.

Prices, contents and availability subject to change without notice.

FOR MORE INFORMATION, SEE YOUR LOCAL MUSIC DEALER, OR WRITE TO:

HAL•LEONARD®
CORPORATION
7777 W. BLUEMOUND RD. P.O. BOX 13819 MILWAUKEE, WI 53213

www.halleonard.com

0516